God Bless U. Don

Jose [illegible]

Sep 1 2007

Single Mother Of Five

By

Rose Joshua (Ph.D.)

Edited By: ***Toyin Souza***

Calgary, Alberta, Canada

Dr. Rose Joshua: Single Mother of Five

Scripture Quotations are from The Online King James Version of the Bible published by the Genesis Networks:

http://www.genesis.net.au/~bible/kjv/index/

National Library of Canada Cataloguing in Publication

Joshua, Rose, 1965-

Single mother of five / by Rose Joshua; edited by Toyin Souza.

Includes bibliographical references.

ISBN 0-9689300-1-8

1. Single mothers--Religious life. 2. Single mothers--Life skills guides.

I. Souza, Toyin, 1972- II. Title.

BV4529.18.J67 2003 248.8'431 C2003-906522-7

Knowledge Sky International, Inc.

Calgary, AB. Canada.

(403)-630-9697

http://www.knowledgesky.com

Printed in Canada by Blitzprint - www.blitzprint.com

Single Mother Of Five

By

Rose Joshua (Ph.D.)

Edited By: ***Toyin Souza***

Calgary, Alberta, Canada

Table of Contents

Dedication

1. To my parents, brothers and sisters, for forgiving me and sticking with me through thick and thin:

My Dad:

Prof. C. N. Anyanwu (B.A. Ph.D.) (1936 – 2001)

My Mum:

Mrs. E. A. N. Anyanwu (B.Sc.)

My brothers:

Dr. E. B. Anyanwu (M.B.B.S., M.D. Pediatrics)

Mr. C. E. Anyanwu (B.Sc., M.Sc.)

My sisters:

Mrs. O. M. Emeka-Egwim (B.Sc. M.Sc.)

Mrs. A. J. Arimah (B.Sc., M.Sc., M.I.S.)

Mrs. I. H. Chimezie (B.Pharm.)

Miss. E. M. Anyanwu (B.Sc.)

2. To my children, Jerry, Peace, Emmanuel, Faith, and Gabrielyn.

3. To all abused women: May the Lord Himself deliver you from bondage, and help you to walk in victory; Amen.

Acknowledgements

I am grateful to members of the All Nations Full Gospel Church, Toronto, and All Nations Full Gospel Church, Calgary, for helping me to my feet, for pulling me out of the pit of depression, and for teaching me to depend on the power of God to improve my life. I thank you for being my support pillars, shoulders to cry on, and prayer partners. Particularly, I want to thank Rev. (Dr.) & Mrs. Sam and Rose Donkor, Rev. & Mrs. Ebow and Hannah Essel, Dr. & Mrs. Gyimah, Prof. & Mrs. Mensah, Rev. & Mrs. Acheampong, Rev. Adu-Bobie, Rev. & Mrs. Dartey, Rev. & Mrs. Armson, Rev. & Mrs. Twum-Barimah, Rev. Christine Mears, and Rev. Abena Yeboah.

I also thank the Owerri Community in Toronto, and Nigerian Canadian Association of Calgary. I thank Mr. Arnold Ingelson and the wonderful teachers and staff at Cedarbrae School, Calgary: Linda Flanagan, Joanne Finlayson, Olga Fraser, Wendy Dobos, Treena Gryschuk, Patty Toner, Jean Peabody, Jane Washenfelder, Kerry Green, Donna Brosh, Diane Campbell, Deborah Ling, Bev Deisinger, Noreen MacMillan, Nancy Stowell, Mat Peters, Debbie Johnston, Margaret Archer, Heather Lamoureux, Fred Conrad, and Margaret Lammiman, Deb MacNaughton, Juanita Ramdewar, and Barb Sargeant. They have been very supportive, and have created an excellent partnership with me in my children's education.

I thank my able editor and sister, Toyin Souza, for the many hours she spent editing my work. I thank Mark Steinfeld for being a father to me, believing in me, and teaching me many things I know about persistence and hard work.

I am immeasurably thankful to my Mum, brothers and sisters (listed on the dedication page), for standing by me through thick and thin. They gave me the strength I needed to go on.

Finally, I thank my *Happy Gang*, my children Jerry, Peace, Emmanuel, Faith, and Gabby. Without them, this book would never have been written. I thank them for always being there for me, for their understanding, and for the excellent spirits that they have to love their Mum no matter what, and to love and walk in the ways of God. I love you, my babies.

Preface

The life of Dr. Rose Joshua is one that brings a lot of joy to our hearts, and one that we know will challenge everyone to a close walk with God Himself. Her story is one that clearly testifies to the ability of God to heal broken hearts, and to bring a faithful child to the success and dreams of her heart.

We met Dr. Joshua when she first came to All Nations Full Gospel Church in 1997, and since then we've seen the touch of God upon her life, and how she has been used of God to challenge men and women to depend on the direction of God to achieve their dreams.

Dr. Joshua has a powerful story to tell. She targets single mothers all over the world, but the insights she presents will be profoundly helpful to everyone – that God is able to walk with you, help you pick up the pieces of your life, and turn your mourning into laughter. She is a living example of this divine plan of God for your life.

Events in our world today indicate that people have allowed themselves to stray from the love of God, and unfortunately it's the women and children who suffer the most. In this predicament, God makes it clear that everyone who is heavy laden should bring their burdens to Him, so He can lift up, heal and comfort the afflicted, and give them joy, peace, and safety.

We challenge you to read this book – it will transform your life and shed the light for a better tomorrow for you and your children

Rev. (Dr.) Sam Donkor / Rev. (Mrs.) Rose Donkor
Senior Pastors,
All Nations Full Gospel Church
(North America, Europe, Africa)

Chapter 1. Introduction: Broken Hearts, Dashed Dreams

"Now all these happened to them as examples, and they were written for our admonition, upon whom the ends of the ages have come. Therefore let him who thinks he stands take heed lest he fall. No temptation has overtaken you except such as is common to man; but God is faithful, who will not allow you to be tempted beyond what you are able, but with the temptation will also make the way of escape, that you may be able to bear it." *(I Corinthians 10:11-13)*

"Blessed be the God and Father of our Lord Jesus Christ, the Father of mercies and God of all comfort, who comforts us in all our tribulation, that we may be able to comfort those who are in any trouble, with the comfort with which we ourselves are comforted by God. For as the sufferings of Christ abound in us, so our consolation also abounds through Christ." *(II Corinthians 1:3-5)*

I give thanks to my Lord Almighty, and to Jesus Christ, for the opportunity to write this book, and to pass on some of the insights I have gained in the last several years to several other people who might encounter similar situations as I did, or people who are in these situations at the moment. I have come across many who have asked me over and over again: "How do you do it?" "Don't you ever feel tired?" "You must be some superwoman", "You deserve a medal!" and so on.

In this book I am speaking to both a general audience, and a specific audience. Generally, I am speaking to the person, male or female, who has been wronged or betrayed and needs to deal with the emotions accruing from that betrayal. Specifically, I am speaking to the single mother who is hurting and wondering within her heart, "Where do I go from here? How do I deal with the emotional state I am in?"

I believe that the Lord has prepared me for such a time as this, to work with women everywhere, who have been hurt, to help soothe their pain, and to give them hugs of comfort. It is true that when one has gone through pain, he or she is better able to understand the pain of someone else at some other time. I have gone through the pain of marital betrayal and battery, and I am going through life as a single mother of five children. So it is quite natural for me to see myself in the shoes of other single women, and to identify with their pain.

It is also true that when a person is in pain, he or she is better able to *listen* to counsel from someone who is either in the same situation, or has gone through a similar situation before. As a result, I know that women everywhere will identify with the discussions I present in this book, because they will recognize that I've *been there* myself.

For the most part, I have addressed several issues that interplay in my daily life: joy, sadness, fatigue, love, and hope. The central theme of my life is to serve the Lord Jesus Christ, for in Him I live, and move, and have my being. Without Him, I would have been long gone, "six feet below ground level". But the Lord, whom I serve, is merciful, and faithful, and is able to make Himself strong on behalf of all those that trust in Him.

One reason I have written this book is to speak to the lives of women everywhere, who are laboring under the yoke of broken homes and relationships. My purpose is to encourage each of these women to focus on the things that really matter, to pick up the pieces and move on in strength and victory, and to hand everything over to the only One who can keep the delicate balance of our daily lives: the Lord Jesus Christ.

Many of us struggle on our own, and fail, naturally. In this book, I have presented to you that only the strength of the Almighty God can help us cope with the daily challenges of raising children in a single-mother home.

Children are a heritage from the Lord, and it is only the Lord who can give us the wisdom and resources to cater properly to the many-faced needs of these children. It is enough trouble to raise a child in a "complete" home, so to say, where there is a father and a mother. However, humanly speaking, it is much more trouble to deal with the absence of a father from a child's daily life. How can we deal with that successfully? Only the Lord can show us the way.

I have included several scriptures that have been encouraging to me. These are words written from the Lord's dictation into our spirits, and I hope that you will dig into the word to find daily strength and encouragement.

I want to thank the Lord for the five gifts He has graciously given me: Jerry, Peace, Emmanuel, Faith, and Gabrielyn. Without them, this book would never have been written. And without their love, hugs, kisses, and thousands of "I love you and I like you, Mum", I would not have had the mental state to look forward to life. God bless you, my babies.

Broken hearts, dashed dreams

> ***"The Spirit of the Lord God is upon Me, because the Lord has anointed Me to preach good tidings to the poor; He has sent Me to heal the brokenhearted, to proclaim liberty to the captives, and the opening of the prison to those who are bound; to proclaim the acceptable year of the Lord, and the day of vengeance of our God; to comfort all who mourn, to console those who mourn in Zion, to give them beauty for ashes, the oil of joy for mourning, the garment of praise for the spirit of heaviness; that they may be called trees of righteousness, the planting of the Lord, that He may be glorified".*** *(Isaiah 61:1-3)*

Nobody ever dreams of having a broken marriage. As a young girl, I did have fantasies based on "happily ever after" stories like "Cinderella", "Snow White", "The Frog Prince", "Rapunzel", and many more. These stories planted some form of utopia in my mind, that some day, I would find a "charming prince", fall in love with him in some magical way, get married, and live "happily ever after". Many women of our time will admit to having such fantasies.

What I did not think about in my childish utopia was that reality is quite different from some of these fairy fantasies. Reality involves human personalities, human behavior, differences in backgrounds, psychology, upbringing, love and hate, everyday hassles, childbearing and childrearing pains, misunderstandings, communication issues, negotiations, suspicions, possessiveness, jealousy, jobs, financial problems, bills, debts, peer pressure, family pressure, internal struggles, and the many, many different facets of life in general, which we begin to face as we grow up.

When two people come together in marriage, the different backgrounds begin to manifest; they must then be blended tactfully for the benefit of the marriage and for the advancement or improvement of the personalities of each spouse. If this blending is not achieved, for whatever reason, the marriage is headed for the rocks and ultimate breakup; or worse still, mutual enmity under a deceptively covered-up façade.

I have a friend who likes to say that some people are divorced and live in separate houses while some are divorced and live in the same house. I'm not sure which is better. It is definitely more correct to say that neither is good, and both result from the fact that two people's personalities have not blended into the oneness, resulting in emotional and physical breakup.

In the event of a physical breakup that involves children, a situation where spouses separate and reside in different locations, the big question becomes that of coping with life as a single parent. Raising a child is a very challenging project, one that demands every resource in a parent, and which also (hopefully) builds that parent's virtues as the parent-child relationship develops.

A mother deals with a child differently from a father. Based on psychological tendencies, a couple ***should*** deal with their children in complementary ways. It is not always the fact that the mother is the 'soft' one, whatever that means. Sometimes, a father is milder in his interaction with the children than a mother. In most cases, however, a father is the major disciplinarian in the home.

Whichever model is represented in a home, a child needs the balance of love and tenderness on the one hand, and strict discipline on the other. These all come together to shape the child's complete psychology, and help to shape the child into a socially balanced citizen that will contribute positively to his or her nation and others around.

When any of the parents is missing from a child's everyday life, an imbalance is created that goes a long way to determining the path led by the child in the future, for life. A portion of this book deals with that imbalance, and how a mother in particular can redirect her child away from the statistical stereotype of a would-have-been unbalanced child.

The children of a single-mother home do not need to be unbalanced. They can have a wholesome and perfectly sound psychology, and can be great successes in their lives. They can affect the world with very positive contributions, ... that is, if the mother does her homework well...

When I got married in the spring of 1991, it was with high hopes, fantastic dreams, and a bright outlook for the future. However, things did go wrong as they always will, and when I was forced to flee my home in 1997, *five children later*, the topmost question on my mind was: how on earth am I going to take care of these children all by myself? It was a journey into an unknown that was plagued with fear both for myself and for my five very young children.

As much as possible, I will not dwell on the things that went wrong. This is because there are millions of single mothers in the world today, with different "scenarios" of things that did go wrong. Dwelling on things that went wrong will open (sometimes mortal) wounds that should better be left to heal. On the other hand, these millions of women, including myself, face a singular challenge: *where do I go from here, and how?*

We've got to march on!

In this book, therefore, I discuss several aspects of this common question. It is my hope that the ideas I have presented in this book will assist and encourage you, and help you on the long journey of overcoming "the evil that people do". For, indeed, the Lord desires for us to be healed. That is why Jesus came! He came that we may be healed, that we may be comforted, and that our sadness may be turned into joy, our ashes to beauty!

He has given us:

> ***"... beauty for ashes, the oil of joy for mourning, the garment of praise for the spirit of heaviness; that [we] might be called trees of righteousness, the planting of the Lord, that He might be glorified. And [we] shall build the old wastes, [we] shall raise up the former desolations, and [we] shall repair the waste cities, the desolations of many generations"*** *(Isaiah 61: 3, 4)*

Arise, and let us rebuild ourselves, that the enemy will not see us and say,

> ***"Ah, so would we have it! ... We have swallowed her up."*** *(Psalms 35:25)*

If anyone would attempt to write about the pains suffered by just one woman in the hands of a man who hates her, there would not be an end to that book. Therefore attempting to represent the pain of millions of suffering women would be an impossible task.

In this book, I have taken the focus away from the cause of your pain. Rather, I have focused on the healing process – how to deal with the pain in an effective and positive manner, and how we can channel the energy from that pain and suffering, into a beautiful testimony for ourselves and for our children, with the help of the Lord Jesus Christ.

My aim is that everyone who reads this book will be challenged to hold on to God and take a turn for the positive. It is normal for a suffering person, especially a single mother with children, to give up hope, quit, throw in the towel, or allow depression to take over. I want to challenge you to the "supernormal", away from the expectation of onlookers, away from the stereotype that society has created about single women, and into a life of victory that only the Lord Jesus Christ can help you walk into.

My theme for this book is: ***It is possible!***

> ***For with God, nothing shall be impossible.*** *(Luke 1:37)*

Shaping the future

To shape a child is to shape the world. The normal mental state of a suffering person is to focus on the immediate environment and circumstances, and not think about the future. Typically, a single mother will give up hope, after looking at her ***current*** situation. The normal fear is: "how in the world can I make it?"

However, we need to step away from what we can do as individuals and as humans, and focus on what the Lord Jesus Christ can do in our lives and with our lives. Each of us has ***so much*** potential that if we even tried a little, we would shock ourselves by the things we can do! We need to hold on to God, and trust that with Him, we can make it through the jungle of confusion, doubts and inadequacies.

We also need to think about the future of our children. Those kids have so much going for them, if we stop to ponder on it, it would blow our minds! ***If nothing else, a single mother must not give up on the possible greatness of her children.*** We must arise and make our children the leaders of tomorrow! Undoubtedly, this is not an easy task, but it can be achieved, not by hopelessness and despair, but by courage and hard work.

We need to look to the future and the amazing possibilities that lie ahead of us. We must make up our minds to work with God, and let Him use us to attain things that we thought were unachievable, to get to heights that we thought were unreachable, and to make ourselves the super heroines of the future generation. Impossible? Think again. Remember: with God, nothing is impossible.

Dealing with the unknown

Of course it is difficult to leap into the unknown. People say that the devil you know is much "safer" than the angel you don't. It seems to make sense until we realize that no matter how much we philosophize, we really don't know what lies ahead, and we really don't have control over it. However, I must quickly add that there is one Person who does – the Lord Jesus Christ. If we put our daily frailty into His hands, He'll lead us through the jungle. I am shortsighted, but He sees the future, for indeed, He

> ***"… declares the end from the beginning, and from ancient times the things that are not yet done…"*** *(Isaiah 46:10)*

Are you afraid to dream? Think about what you could do, and think that if you let life just pass you by, you will look back only with regret. Each of us has a peculiar opportunity to reach for the skies. And if you think you can't do it, I challenge you with the Scripture that says,

> ***"I can do all things only through Jesus Christ who gives me strength."*** *(Philippians 4:13)*

A good old song says, "My God knows the way through the wilderness; all I have to do is to follow." I want to encourage you, as you read this book, to cast aside all the doubts you have about yourself. You've got to forge ahead, leave the past behind, and press forward into a new life of open doors with God. As you reach forward, you'll find that the doors will begin to open before you. Victory awaits you – but you must move forward into it. You've got to take the first step.

Chapter 2. First Things First: Are you Born Again?

"Jesus answered and said to [Nicodemus], Verily, verily I say unto you, except a man be born again, he cannot see the kingdom of God." *(John 3:16)*

"For by grace are you saved through faith; and that not by yourselves, it is the gift of God; not by works, lest any man should boast." *(Ephesians 2:8, 9)*

"And as it is appointed unto man once to die, but after this the judgment: so Christ was once offered to bear the sins of many; and unto them that look for Him shall He appear the second time without sin unto salvation." *(Hebrews 9:27, 28)*

"For we must all appear before the judgment seat of Christ; that everyone may receive the things done in he has done in his body, according to what he has done, whether it is good or bad." *(II Corinthians 5:10)*

"Be not deceived: God is not mocked; for whatsoever a man sows, that shall he also reap. For he that sows to the flesh shall of the flesh reap corruption, but he that sows to the Spirit shall of the Spirit reap life everlasting." *(Galatians 6:7-9)*

"But she that lives in pleasure is dead while she lives." *(I Timothy 5:6)*

Without a shadow of doubt, the only power that has kept me alive today, and with my "(mental) head on my (physical) head" so to say, without ending up in a psychiatric hospital, is the Lord Jesus Christ Himself. If I wasn't connected to the Father of Lights, I would have been groping around in darkness, and going around in circles until the devil has had his field day with me, with my children, and anything else he can lay hands on! This is because ***the devil, as a roaring lion, is going to and fro, looking for people he can devour*** *(I Peter 5:8).*

As my Pastor says, if you don't have God as your protection, the devil would eat you for breakfast, lunch and supper! That is so true especially for a single woman with children.

Single mothers and their children are very easy prey for the devil; he'll bring temptation to a confused woman, and once he's got the woman, the children are pieces of cake. This is so sad but true. However, if you have the Lord God Almighty solidly behind you, the devil will not even come near. You need God's divine cover from that bully devil by being born again.

You need to be born again

Putting it straight and simple, to effectively survive and succeed in our world today, you need the strength, light, direction, and protection that only God can provide. No matter how smart you are, there are several reasons why you need God: the earth is older than you; you don't know tomorrow from today; you do not have sole control over the events of the very next minute; you have no control whatsoever over the breath in your lungs; neither do you have any idea how or when you will leave this earth. What more compelling justification do you need to look to the Lord who made you, for salvation and daily direction?

There are several arguments in our contemporary age, which attempt to defy the need for God, or for any divine guidance except for thoughts from within man himself. Unfortunately, those who present these arguments forget their own frailties and 'luck', so to say. For example, from time to time we see people down the roads who have cases of mental disorder. Did they choose to be that way? Of course not! Can their lives be changed? Yes, only by the power of God. This means that those who have their "minds together" are living by the grace of God, and should be thankful for it.

Again, I like to say to those who argue that "there is no life after death", or that "once you die, that's the end", to think that it would be too late by the time they get to the grave. When you suddenly realize at death that there is really life after death, it would unfortunately be too late to undo your philosophy.

You see, God has actually given us a natural glimpse into the spiritual world. Some people say that "men learn to die by sleeping". An odd saying, but think about dreamland, and the things that occur to us in our dreams or nightmares. If a man could have interactions while asleep, what prevents interactions while dead? Moreover, if we could dream and sometimes the events of those dreams manifest immediately in our wakefulness, what prevents the manifestation of heaven or hell in our death? Think about it…

People can be quite ironic. For example, we take life insurance policies so that when we die, our loved ones can take care of our funerals, and hopefully have some money to spare for settling any applicable estates. Also, we take these life insurance policies quite early in life, because "you never know". If we take life insurance for the people we leave behind, isn't it ironic that many of us don't take spiritual life insurance for ourselves?

If a man is born again, he has taken that spiritual life insurance. Even if you buy the most expensive life insurance policy in the world, if you neglect your spiritual life insurance, you have done yourself the greatest disfavor of all times.

> ***For what shall it profit a man if he shall gain the world and lost his own soul? And what shall a man give in exchange for his soul?*** *(Mark 8:36-37)*

The bottom line is this: there is life after death. We must not allow ourselves to be deceived by ignorant people who will persuade by vain words, to ignore this fact that stares us right in the face. We get an interesting illustration in the Scriptures, as Jesus tells the dramatic story of the rich man and Lazarus:

> ***"There was a certain rich man who was dressed in purple and fine linen, and fared sumptuously everyday: and there was a certain beggar named Lazarus, who was laid at his gate, full of sores, and desiring to be fed with the crumbs that fell from the rich man's table: moreover, the dogs came and licked his sores. And it came to pass that the beggar died, and was carried by the angels into Abraham's bosom; the rich man also died and was buried; And in hell he lifted up his eyes, being in torments, and saw Abraham afar off, and Lazarus in his bosom; And he cried and said, Father***

Abraham, have mercy on me, and send Lazarus, that he may dip the tip of his finger in water, and cool my tongue; for I am tormented in this flame. But Abraham said, son, remember that you in your lifetime received your good things, and likewise Lazarus evil things: but now he is comforted, but you are tormented. And beside all this, between us and you there is a great gulf fixed: so that those who want to pass from here to you cannot; neither can those who want to come from there pass to us. Then [the rich man] said, I pray you therefore, that you would send him to my father's house: for I have five brothers; that he may testify to them, lest they also come to this place of torment. Abraham said to him, they have Moses and the prophets; let them [listen to] them. And he said, No, Father Abraham; but if one went to them from the dead, they would repent. And [Abraham] said to him: if they do not listen to Moses and the prophets, neither would they be persuaded even if one rose from the dead. *" (Luke 16:19-31)*

It is easy to flagrantly deny the existence of God. But we have had renowned prophets and preachers in our time – think of the countless preachers in our neighborhoods, on television, in books, on tapes, on CD's and now, me, Rose Joshua!

You really have no excuse to ignore the message of salvation. But what are you going to do with that message? My persuasion to you is to turn your life over to the Lord Jesus Christ for salvation and peace. That is the beginning of victory and wisdom. That is the beginning of your ability to cope with the challenges and struggles of raising children as a single woman. Jesus is the Lord of wisdom, and ***the fear of God is the beginning of wisdom*** *(Psalms 111:10, Proverbs 9:10).*

How would you feel if you knew what to do when you are faced with every situation? Well, you can have that internal light, showing you what to do, through the guidance of God from inside you when you are born again. Start from here – there's no better way.

What does it mean to be born again?

The human control caucus is a layered structure of three closely interwoven entities: the spirit, the soul, and the body.

Of course, what we all see with our eyes is the external body of individuals around us. The *soul* is the seat of emotions – fear, anger, happiness, sadness, love, hate. The *spirit* is the connection between the individual and supernatural powers, specifically, God or the devil.

Unknown to many, the spirit is the most important part of the human tripartite nature. When a child is born, however, the spirit is initially disconnected from God. This is due to the sin of our first father and mother (Adam and Eve) in the Garden of Eden. Because of their sin, the entire human race is born with 'original' sin as some call it. This means that we are born in alienation from God, that is, we are born spiritually dead! David confirms this by lamenting in Psalms 51:5:

> ***"Behold, I was shaped in iniquity, and in sin did my mother conceive me".***

Paul further confirms this in Romans 3: 10 and 23:

"... there is none righteous, no not one...", and "... all have sinned and come short of the glory of God."

In order to reunite our spirits to God, there needs to be a spiritual birth of each person. The first birth is the natural birth from our mother's wombs. The second and more important is the birth of our spirits to God through Jesus Christ. This is why it's called being born 'again', signifying a second birth, not naturally, but spiritually.

Jesus explained this concept to Nicodemus when he said,

> ***"... Verily, verily I say unto you, except a man be born again, he cannot see the kingdom of God"*** *(John 3:3)*

Naturally, Nicodemus did not understand, which was why he asked if being born again meant going back into his mother's womb. Jesus explained that

"... except a man be born of water and of the Spirit, he cannot enter into the kingdom of God." (John 3:5)

We know that all men are born of *water.* The 'water' birth is delivery from our mothers' wombs, where a child is taken out of his or her 'water bag' or amniotic sac. However, natural birth is not sufficient to enter into the kingdom of God. We need the second birth, which is that by the Holy Spirit of God, where a person reconnects his or her spirit to the Spirit of God and is born again.

What if you ignore the call to salvation?

Being human as we are, it is quite tempting to ignore the message of salvation as baloney, or just another joke, or under all sorts of excuses. However, there are dire consequences for not heeding the voice of God when He calls. First, we must understand that there is a heaven and a hell, and that there will be a judgment of the dead. At the judgment, those who are Christians, who follow the call of Jesus Christ, will go to heaven; others who ***chose*** to do things their own way, who do not heed the call of Jesus Christ, will be cast away into hell.

> ***"When the Son of Man shall come in His glory, and all the holy angels with Him, then shall He sit upon the throne of His glory; and before Him shall be gathered all nations, and He shall separate them one from another, as a shepherd divides his sheep from the goats: and He shall set the sheep on His right hand, and the goats on the left. Then shall the King say to them on His right hand, 'Come, ye blessed of my Father, inherit the kingdom prepared for you from the foundation of the world: …' … Then shall He say also to them on the left hand, 'Depart from me, you cursed, into everlasting fire, prepared for the devil and his angels …'…"*** *(Matthew 25: 31 – 46)*

Also, let us take the spiritual encouragement in Hebrews, where the Scripture warns that we must not take the free salvation of God lightly or for granted.

> ***"Therefore we ought to give the more earnest heed to the things which we have heard, lest at any time we should let them slip. For if the word spoken by angels was steadfast, and every transgression and disobedience received a just recompense of reward; how shall we***

> ***escape if we neglect so great salvation; which at the first began to be spoken by the Lord [Jesus Christ], and was confirmed to us by those who heard Him.”*** *(Hebrews 2: 1-3)*

Church attendance is not enough

Is being born again equivalent to attending church? Church attendance is definitely important for every child of God, but it is not equivalent to being born again. There are people who attend church weekly, but who still commit atrocities in the name of God. But God is not mocked. He knows those who are truly His, and in the last day, He will separate the good from the bad, the wheat from the chaff, and all will come to light.

> ***“Strive to enter in through the narrow gate; for many, I say to you, will seek to enter in, and shall not be able. When the master of the house is risen up and has shut the door, and you begin to stand outside and knock at the door saying, ‘Lord, Lord, open to us’, and He shall answer and say to you, ‘I don’t know where you come from’. Then you shall say, ‘we have eaten and drunk in your presence, and you have taught in our streets’. But He shall say, ‘I tell you, I don’t know where you come from; depart from me, all you*** workers of iniquity***.’ There shall be weeping and gnashing of teeth, when you shall see Abraham, and Isaac, and Jacob, and all the prophets in the kingdom of God, and you, cast out.”*** *(Luke 13: 24 – 28)*

The Lord knows those who ‘work iniquity’, even though they look perfect in church every Sunday morning. Church attendance is therefore not sufficient in itself. Attending church without doing the will of God by being born again is like putting the cart before the horse, or building a house without a foundation.

The bottom line is this: you need to be born again. You need the strength of God to face the hustle, bustle and confusions of your daily life, and you need the assurance of God for the life to come. All persuasions against this are fallacy, and will lead to nothing but eternal regret.

<u>When is a good time to be born again?</u>

> ***"... behold now is the accepted time; behold now is the day of salvation."*** *(II Corinthians 6:2)*
>
> ***"Wherefore as the Holy Ghost says, today if you will hear His voice, do not harden your hearts, as in the provocation, in the day of temptation in the wilderness."*** *(Hebrews 3: 7-8, 15)*

Today is the day of salvation; tomorrow may be too late. Last Christmas, I watched a movie at my church, in which a Minister preached the message of salvation. Then I saw different members of the congregation and how they reacted to the message. Some accepted the message; some outrightly blocked their minds from receiving, and some argued it all away. I remember watching the case of a beautiful young lady, in her early twenties, who argued that "life still has much to offer; I'm still young; I need to ***enjoy*** life (whatever that means)..." and so on, and so forth. Then I watched as she left the service, drove away, and had a head-on collision with a drunk driver. She died on the spot.

Seems quite dramatic but so true in many cases.

Sometimes we think we have all the time in the world. We want to get a job first, then we want to marry, then have kids, then a car, then investment, then we want to leave it until we are old, ... But again, we have no idea when the time of death will come. Of course while we live, it's important to keep busy and to achieve things, and to influence people around us positively, but no one knows when Mr. Death will come to collect the soul.

And so, procrastinating salvation is a deadly game, as illustrated by the case of the lady in the movie I watched. Now is the best time.

<u>How can you be born again?</u>

Simply by asking Jesus Christ into your heart, to come in and cleanse your heart from all unrighteousness, and to make you God's child. Jesus is waiting for you to ask Him into your heart:

> ***Behold I stand at the door and knock; if any man hears my voice and opens the door, I will come in to him and sup with him and he with me.*** *(Revelation 3:20)*

Jesus says again in several scriptures:

> ***I am the way, the truth and the life; no man comes to the Father except through me*** *(John 14:6)*

> ***I am the door; if any man enters by me, he shall be saved, and shall go in and out and find pasture*** *(John 10:9)*

> ***I am the good shepherd; the good shepherd gives his life for the sheep*** *(John 10:11).* (Jesus died on the cross so that you and I can be saved and go to heaven)

So it is as simple as praying to God, in the name of Jesus Christ, to come into your heart, and making your spirit new and one with His Holy Spirit.

Once you are born again, you become equipped with the spiritual strength to face life, especially that of a single mother. You will attend church as usual, but now there is a reason in your heart to augment the life in your heart with fellowship with other Christians in church.

Not just for you, but for your children

Every single mother, who has the lives of children in her hands, needs to be born again, not just for herself, but also for her children. A child needs love, protection, and guidance, but we cannot truly give love unless the God of love lives in our hearts. We cannot give protection because it's not in us to give, really! It's only the Lord who protects His own. Also, we cannot give guidance because we do not know what will happen tomorrow, and we have no control over the affairs of our everyday lives. We can work hard, but there are many factors over which we have no control. For example, how are we to know that a drunk driver will not hit us if we went on Highway 90 as opposed to going on Highway 75? It takes the Lord Himself who will gently lead you. Remember His promise that says:

> ***He shall feed His flock like a shepherd: He shall gather***

> ***the lambs with His arm, and carry them in His bosom, and shall gently lead those that are with young.*** *(Isaiah 40:11)*

Because you are *with young (*that is, you have young children to cater for), the Lord will lead you gently. But you need to give Him the chance to do so. Being born again is the beginning of the journey. Pray to God today, … now; ask the Lord Jesus Christ to come into your heart, then hit the road of being a single mother with the only One who can truly help you to succeed.

Chapter 3. Build a Strong Support Community

"Behold, how good and how pleasant it is for brethren to dwell together in unity!" *(Psalm 133:1)*

"I was glad when they said me, 'Let us go into the house of the Lord.' Our feet have been standing within your gates, O Jerusalem! Jerusalem is built as a city that is compact together, where the tribes go up, the tribes of the Lord, to the Testimony of Israel, to give thanks to the Name of the Lord." *(Psalms 122:1-4)*

"Here am I and the children whom the Lord has given me! We are for signs and wonders in Israel from the Lord of hosts, Who dwells in Mount Zion." (Isaiah *8:18)*

One day in 1999, I was listening to a radio broadcast on social issues, and the speakers revealed something that many of us have known all along: that a child who grows in a large extended family has a higher chance of success than those who grow in a small, somewhat secluded nuclear relationship. Building a large community around you is not only important for you as a single Mum; it is moreso important for your children. This is because the benefits you get from a community base will surely reflect in the relationships picked up by your children. In turn, the community will help to satisfy their varying needs, and shape their futures.

What is a community?

By 'community', I do not necessarily mean the political or local area in which you live. According to the Merriam-Webster English Dictionary, a community could be defined in many ways, including the following:

> ***"a unified body of individuals as a state or commonwealth", "the people with common interests living in a particular area, or broadly, the area itself", "an interacting population of various kinds of individuals in a common location", "a group of people with a common characteristic or interest living together within a larger society", or "a body of persons ... Having a common history or common social ... Interests", "a common character: likeness", "fellowship"...***

It is clear that the central keyword in "community" is the word "common". A community, therefore, is a group that, although geographically dispersed in primary residence, frequently comes together to share common interests and to interact on a common plain.

Start with Your Own Family (If Possible)

Of course the first place to look when you need comfort and solace from outside your home, is your extended family – parents, cousins, other close relatives. If you have a supportive extended family, count yourself blessed. This is because they have known you ever since you were a child; they know your history, and are always there for you no matter what.

I praise the Lord Almighty for my

parents, Professor & Mrs. Clement and Eunice Anyanwu. Although I got married without parental consent (quite a different story, and definitely one of the roots of my marital problems), when I really needed help, they were there for me. Even when others thought that my parents were foolish to assist me, they both came to my aid. I also thank God for my brothers and sisters. They joined hands together and ran to my aid without my calling, and they've been unequivocally supportive ever since. With a family like that, you can never be alone.

However, please note that not every family is supportive. In fact, many single women face life all alone because neither their extended family, nor their ex's extended family (naturally) render them any support. People do have different reasons for turning their backs on their loved ones. For example, some extended family members are just 'waiting' for a marriage to break up so they can say "I told you so", or "I warned her but she wouldn't listen", and so on. If you have family like that, you really don't need that extra hassle – ignore them and strike out for survival on your own.

However, in addition to your extended family, you also need other supportive community that will help you to grow in different dimensions. This is very important for the children.

My Church Community Is Excellent!

With all gratitude to the Lord Jesus Christ, and without any shadow of doubt, I believe that my life would not have been the same if the Lord had not led me gently by the hand, to the Christian community in All Nations Full Gospel Church, Toronto, and now to All Nations Full Gospel Church in Calgary, Alberta (henceforth referred to as "All Nations", for short).

I was introduced to the church by my brother- and sister-in-law, Mike and Ebun Arimah, in the summer of 1996. At that time, I was spiritually out of touch, and had not attended a good Christian service for several years. I did belong to a so-called 'church', but I knew it was a mockery of God's Name and holy ordinances.

Mike and Ebun encouraged me to come to All Nations, and I went. From the moment I walked into the church sanctuary, and heard the praises of the people of God flowing up to heaven, I knew that was the place for me. After my first attendance, I did fellowship in All Nations off and on for about a year, and eventually settled down to full-time attendance after I fled my home in 1997.

Your Community Must Make You Feel Welcome

One of the mission statements of All Nations is to 'make everyone feel loved and accepted'. If you are in a group or community in which you are not loved or accepted for who you are, please pack up and find a better group. You don't want to stay with high-nosed or snobbish individuals who think they are better or more privileged than you. Who needs that high-horse attitude?

Also, you want your children to feel psychologically

able to deal with other children in your community or social group. If the kids cannot blend with the others, you may start thinking of finding a group in which your kids will feel welcome and positively challenged rather than insulted or reminded about negative things.

In All Nations, I felt welcome right away! After that first service, Mike and Ebun introduced me to the Senior Pastors and Founders of All Nations, Dr. & Mrs. Sam and (Mama) Rose Donkor. At that time, I was expecting my last child, Gabby. Pastor Donkor pointed at my belly and said jovially, "I see you are cooking". I laughed and said, "Yes, I am, Pastor". He asked me if that was my first child, and I replied that this was my fifth. He replied, "Wow, you beat us to it!" (the Donkors have four children). Mama Rose was standing there beside him and welcomed me with her characteristic smiles. They came across as very pleasant people, and on our way back home, I promised Mike and Ebun that I would surely return.

The remarkable thing about All Nations was not only that the Pastor and his wife were jovial and welcoming; the people also stopped to say "Hello". I knew no one in the congregation except Mike and Ebun, but several people came by, shook my hands, smiled, chit-chatted, and helped me feel very, very welcome. I loved them from that first day!

Go For a Close-Knit Community

The central focus of looking for a community or group to associate with, is to find close friends with whom you can relate, share ideas, and get the strength and motivation to move on with your life as a single mother. One negative thing about several communities is that they are so large that one can easily feel lost even though one is surrounded by a lot of people! For example, it is possible to attend a large community function and just be another face in the crowd. After the function, everyone simply disappears. It is not uncommon to see people who have remained depressed or lonely despite their membership of a large community.

What you really need is a community that can organize smaller units of interaction, even if it's a large group. This was one of the things that helped my kids and I settle very quickly in All Nations Full Gospel Church.

At the very core of the organizational structure of All Nations is the Cell Ministry, which makes this church the most far-reaching and community-based church I have ever seen. The Cell organization is such that the Senior Pastor is the leader of the Cell Ministry (and of course, other ministries as well). Each city or municipality has its Regional Touch Pastor (RTP), under whom are Touch Pastors, under whom are cell leaders. Each cell leader has an average cell size of 8 - 10 members. When a cell grows too large, it is split (or "multiplied") to create a new cell.

One of the main purposes of the Cell Ministry is to reach out to individuals *personally*, to touch and attend to their *personal* needs, and to communicate these needs up the pastoral hierarchy, as required, much like the communication chain in the days of Moses. As far as All Nations goes, this hierarchical communication is not bureaucratic at all. All Touch Pastors, their assistants, the Regional Touch Pastor, and even the Senior Pastor, are available 24 hours a day (this is true!), seven days a week. This means that if a cell member is in hospital, the Cell Leader can inform the Touch Pastor at midnight, depending on the gravity of the situation.

After my children and I moved to Etobicoke, Ontario in 1997, my Touch Pastor, Esther Idowu, assigned me my first Cell Leaders: Padmore-Tabi and Mary Gyansah. You may have guessed correctly that cell leadership in All Nations is a partnership between husband and wife. If a man is selected to be Cell Leader, his wife automatically becomes partner in the ministry, and vice-versa. This way, couples can build each other up in the spiritual warfare.

"Uncle Tabi", as we know him, made us feel comfortable right away. The day after we moved in, he came with his wife and TP Esther to pray with us. Esther and Mary brought us food, fruits, and clothing. Uncle Tabi also introduced me to his Assistant, Alberta Birinkorang, and other members of the cell.

At this time, my mother, Mrs. Eunice Ada Anyanwu, was with me and she was very impressed with the way we were made to feel at home. She remarked that these 'people' are real Christians, who ministered to people at their specific points of need. She saw the sense of community we received from the Cell Ministry, and even when she traveled overseas, she made it a point to write several letters to my Cell, to bless them, and to encourage them in the work they were doing.

Your Community Must Build You Up and Challenge You to be Better

One good thing about community is that you can interact with individuals from different backgrounds and experiences, and learn a thing or two. One of the first things I learnt from my interaction with my cell group at All Nations, was how to truly love and care for one another, and how to pray.

For example, after I fled my home, I had no means of transportation, and my children and I went to school and work by bus and train. However, Uncle Tabi took it upon himself to provide us with transportation to and from church for *every* meeting: the church meets on Wednesdays, Fridays and Sundays. This undertaking translated to a lot of sacrifice on his part (time, and gas bills), because at that time, his family had a small two-door Pony, a small car indeed.

Uncle Tabi would make two trips to church, just to pick us up as well as drop off his family. With a distance of about 15km from church, this meant that he traveled back and forth, more than 60km just to attend each service. Fortunately, coming back was sometimes easier because he organized for rides back home after the services. I was so deeply touched by these time and financial sacrifices, and each time I commented on it, Uncle Tabi would reply with enthusiasm, "My sister, don't worry. It's God. We love you, and we want you to be faithful. Don't worry about me. God loves you. Just be faithful." This made a very big impression in my heart. I undertook to pray for Uncle Tabi, that the Lord would bless him with a bigger car, so he would not have to make too many trips. And to God be the glory, the Lord did bless him with a van! One thing I have come to know about the Lord is that He rewards His servants and those who are diligent in His kingdom.

Moreover, Uncle Tabi was a clear example to me of the way the cell ministry works. He was with us all the time, praying with us, challenging us to be faithful. When my children got sick, Uncle Tabi and Auntie Mary (as we called his wife) would come to visit. If they could not make it, they were sure to give us a telephone call.

On one occasion, Gabby was admitted for asthma at the Etobicoke General Hospital. All I did was call Uncle Tabi, and before I knew it, I had got a visit from Touch Pastor Esther Idowu herself, with Tabi, and lots of my cell members as well as other members of the church. The Senior Pastor also called to pray with us. What fellowship! What a great community!

Your Community Must Appeal to the Children

It wouldn't make sense for you to spend a lot of time with a group in which the children do not feel comfortable. Of course I'm not talking about adult groups where you can have quiet personal times with grown-ups at a common intellectual level. I'm referring to the group you have chosen for common therapeutic benefits for you and the children. If they don't get any benefits from that community, it's not worth it.

My children just love to attend All Nations, especially the cell meetings. They get to interact with other children at a close level, meet with the adults in a manner that is more relaxed than the usual environment of solemn Sunday mornings and hasty Sunday afternoons. Cell meetings are informal; everyone gets to give a testimony if they want; my kids love to testify to the goodness of God for helping them with their homework; they love the appreciation (claps) they receive for testifying to God's goodness; all that attention makes them feel good and special.

Most important to the kids were the refreshments after the cell meetings! Kids are very interesting! They have more fun with the cell food than if they had exactly the same things cooked at home! Just sharing the refreshments with more people offered more excitement. Some days when I am extremely tired and unable to attend Cell meetings, my kids would insist they want to go. If I press to find out why they really want to go, 10 times out of 10, they always reply that it is the food!

I thank the Lord for the community in All Nations. Although my kids go to Cell for the food, they definitely get some spiritual uplifting from Cell meetings as well, because after meetings and on our way home, they are able to articulate and discuss some of the issues raised at the meetings.

Your Community Must Build Your Confidence and Trust

I came to All Nations broken, battered, and really hurt; they picked me up, put my pieces together, and nurtured me back to spiritual and mental health, with steadfast dedication and love.

When we first arrived at All Nations, my kids were a frightened bunch. They did not know whom to trust or relate with. Of course, after witnessing several parental fights, and police visits, fear and insecurity became part of their daily lives. As a result, they stuck to me like glue, and would go with me wherever I went (funny, they still want to go with me wherever I go, but they are a lot more independent now).

At that initial stage, leaving them in their Sunday School classes were always a challenge. Gabby, my youngest, would cry and howl so loud that the teachers would quickly come and fetch me for assistance. One clear case that comes to mind is Jerry, who was five years old at that time. When it came time for Sunday school, Jerry would cry and shuffle his feet, and develop 'jelly knees' (you know, the type that makes them crumple on the floor deliberately). I would literally carry him into his class.

One day, Jerry held on to one side of his classroom's doorframe, put the length of his body across the door so that his legs held onto the other side of the door, and he kept howling, "I want to stay with my Mummy! Don’t take me away from my Mummy!!!..." His teacher, Robert, and I tried to pull his hands off the frame, but we couldn't. When he had calmed down a little bit, Robert picked him up, held him to himself and said, "OK, love. It's OK now.

You have nothing to worry about, I'm your friend." Then Robert asked me to leave Jerry with him.

As Jerry himself recounted later, Robert soothed him, sat beside him for the entire duration of the class, held his hands many times, smiled at him, told him how special he was, and said to him many times, "I'm your friend, OK?" After that singular event, Jerry would always go to his class. When Robert had to leave town for some time and Jerry's class got another teacher, Dr. Hammah (popularly called "Uncle Papa"), Jerry initially said he did not want to go to Sunday School because "Uncle Robert is not there anymore". However, when I explained Jerry's situation to Uncle Papa, he treated him specially as well, and Jerry decided to stay. Jerry has loved Sunday School since then, made several friends among his age-mates, and is much more independent.

It's really important that your community helps you to build up confidence and trust in them. With that confidence, you can begin to feel much better about the future and how to handle it. If you are in a community where people are unfriendly or dubious, that does not help at all.

Your Community Must Give You Personal Attention

Although All Nations is a large church, I noticed right away that the Senior Pastor and his wife did pay attention to new members of the congregation. They would call us at home to find out how we were doing. Pastor would stop by the kids, pick them up, tell them "I love you", and pray with them.

After Gabby returned from her last hospitalization for asthma, Pastor Donkor called us to his office, took the child in his arms, prayed for her healing. He commanded the spirit of asthma to leave her. Since then, she has been healed. He also laid hands on Jerry, Peace, Emmanuel and Faith, and asked the Lord to be their father and to heal their hearts. We do owe a lot to those fatherly prayers.

Since we moved to Calgary in 2000, I have seen the same expression of the love of God in All Nations Calgary as well. My Pastor Ebow Essel, his wife Hannah, and the entire congregation, are very loving and caring people. They call us frequently, come to visit, and are definitely there for us whenever we need them. It's a great family to be in!

Apart from the Pastoral chain in the All Nations' Cell Ministry, the congregation is full of really nice and loving folks. There are lots and lots of beloved brothers and sisters in All Nations, who have touched our lives with many gifts and in many different ways – they take it upon themselves to cook us meals, help clean the house, mow the lawn, take the kids out for snacks, and have literally spoilt us so much! Space does not permit me to write everyone's name in here, but they are all chronicled on the tablet of my heart, and my prayer for them always, is that the good Lord, who has used them to touch these little children, will keep their hearts and minds in Christ, and will prosper them abundantly, in Jesus' Name; Amen.

For example, Prof. & Mrs. Mensah adopted me as their daughter, and my kids as their grandchildren. They are an extremely loving couple who have raised several children and grandchildren of their own, and continue to be a mother and father in All Nations. We also have GrandPa and GrandMa Seth Bempong. For some reason, Gabby would always run to GrandPa Seth and shout "GrandMa". To Gabby, once somebody's popular name starts with the word "Grand...", it had to be "GrandMa"! (That's because my Mum lives with us and she's GrandMa of course). Daddy Seth would always give a hilarious belly-laugh from being so enthusiastically called "GrandMa"!

When you get personal attention from your community, you feel truly loved and accepted. This is key to a single Mum's sense of security and belonging in any community. It's also very psychologically beneficial for the children, because they know they have a large extended family of support around them.

Find people you can relate with at a personal level. Don't be afraid or ashamed to receive their free gifts and caring attention. I have found that it is therapeutic to allow yourself to receive all this *tender loving care,* because it will go a long way to helping to build you and the children up, especially in the ability to trust again.

Your Community Must Build Your Self-Esteem

It goes without saying that a good and fairly large community is a growth and healing resource for my children and I. The children do have a great sense of belonging, a knowing of their acceptance, no matter what.

Everyone in the community looks out for them, and do you know what that does to their self-esteem? Shoots it all the way up to the sky! Those kids know that 'Auntie A' or 'Uncle B' loves and cares for them, buys them gifts, calls to find out how they are doing at home, and comes from time to time to visit. They know they have a large family and it is just great! They have lots of places to visit, lots of friends their age, they can share games and toys with their friends, watch movies together, and so on. These kids will not be counted in the statistics of psychologically under-developed children. Never!

You know one other major benefit I get from my community? I can get a break from the children whenever I am stressed out! I have lots of Christian brothers and sisters who are willing to take my children for the weekend, so I could put my feet up and rest! Isn't that great? Sometimes I feel I have even offended some because the kids could not make it to their place quickly enough, since we often have a long line-up of families who have planned to take the kids. Sometimes we have it planned months ahead!

One more thing, the community makes for good discipline as well. Many times, I have told my kids, "If you keep on doing that, I'm gonna have to tell Uncle Kofi, or Uncle Henry". When I say that, they freak out! Not out of fear, but out of a sense of knowing that their discipline comes not only from Mum, but from the large community network. All of a sudden, they behave themselves because they want to maintain a good image with these beloved Uncles and Aunties. It's amazing! On one occasion for instance, Emmanuel wailed and howled simply because I was going to tell Uncle Nnamdi on him! He begged and begged me not to, and promised that he would never misbehave for the rest of his life! Yeah, right! But I understood that was his way of telling me he was sorry.

The effect of community on children is tremendous, since they know that their community, which is like a large extended family, is very much around, and would not tolerate it if they treat their Mum with disrespect, or fail to do their chores around the house, etc. It' very much like the communities we have back home in Africa, where everyone looks out for everyone else's child, and if anyone sees my child misbehaving in the park, they would discipline them without seeking the parent's permission. A great close-knit community is good for the kids; it ensures that we have disciplined leaders for tomorrow.

My Cultural Community

Apart from the church community, while we lived in Toronto we also belonged to our heritage or 'root' community, the Owerri Local Community of Toronto, which is the group of brothers and sisters from my children's hometown in Nigeria. Here in Calgary, we belong to the Nigerian Canadian Association of Calgary. Notice that I'm using the word *belong,* because it's important that your community gives you a sense of *belonging.*

The Owerri group was very helpful to the kids since we spoke our natural language during our monthly meetings, and the kids were able to pick up dialectic words from discussions in the meetings. Here in Calgary, the Nigerian Association organizes natural language classes and career-directed workshops for the children.

My kids always look forward to these community meetings, again because of the great Nigerian dishes that we eat: moin-moin, chin-chin, foo-foo, pounded-yam, egusi, ofe-owerri, ... Lovely food! From the information they get from our community discussions, the kids ask questions about Nigeria: where it is, what it looks like, and the most popular one – "Mum, when can you take us to Nigeria?" Great questions, and it is gratifying, because they know they have a root, and a place where their grandparents still live, and where they have lots and lots of cousins, uncles and aunties!

When I entertain visitors in my home, many of them observe that my kids are assertive, confident, and very much at ease. It has not always been like that. We have come a long way, and it could not have been possible without the excellent community that the Lord has woven us into. This is our family and we love them very, very, very much.

Contribute: Use Your Talents for Your Community

From the foregoing, I cannot over-emphasize the need for a strong community bond for you and the children. I encourage everyone who is "alone with the kids" to seek out a community, preferably a church community. Our Bible-believing churches are filled with loving, experienced people who will work with you to put you back on your feet, and establish excellent relationships with your children. You will no longer need to worry about "how on earth" you are going to raise them. Belonging to a community will help any overworked, overstressed Mum, and also the children.

Believe it or not, the kids are not happy to *always be with Mum*. Sometimes they want to break out, go and play somewhere else, go talk to a friend, or enjoy a different menu for a change. I bet you sometimes hear them say, "Ha, Mum, not tuna again!" or "Mum, why do you *always* make meat loaf?" or "I ***hate*** macaroni and cheese!"

The community around you gives them the opportunity to express themselves. It frees them from boredom, gives them varieties of relationships, activities and menus, and makes your lives together much more at ease.

Finally, finding a community is not always about *receiving* from them; it's also about you *giving* to them. Of course, initially, if you're still struggling to find your feet, the relationship would be one where you receive more than you give, but eventually, there will come a time when you must contribute to your community in order to feel truly fulfilled. Strive for this point, and use your talents and gifts to enrich and give to your community.

Share your experiences, and help other single mothers who may be struggling with things you have overcome in the past. In my case for example, when I speak to a woman in distress, there's a sympathy chord between us, and she is better able to accept encouragement from me than from someone else who has never been through what I have experienced. God will use your experience to help others in your situation, and you can look back and thank Him that the past is not wasted years after all. Go for it, and may God bless our good communities!

Chapter 4. Deal With Important Issues: The 'Me Factor'

Once you have laid the foundation of being born again, connected to the divine strength that comes from God alone, and also immersed yourself and your children into a healthy community, you need to begin to focus on the road back to a normal, healthy life for you and the children.

The 'Me' Factor

God commands us to 'love our neighbors as ourselves'. Therefore the first part of the plan to normalize your life is yourself. You've got to take care of yourself before you can have the physical, emotional, spiritual or mental capability to take care of your children or others around you. So the most important part of that equation is you, what I call the 'me factor'.

When it comes to taking care of yourself, you need to search your soul, and ask a few basic questions. These are some examples I had to deal with:

How has the breakup in my relationship affected me?

Am I emotionally scarred (most of the time, the answer to this question is a big yes)?

Am I mentally able to continue the journey with the children all by myself (the usual answer to this is a 'no')?

Am I financially capable of raising the children on my own (in many cases, the answer to this is no as well)?

Where shall we live? How shall we feed? How shall we pay our bills?

Questions and more questions... These all need answers, and I will address most of them in the rest of this book. However, in this chapter, we must focus on a core or fundamental part of the soul-searching phase: your ***emotional and mental health***. This is because once you have taken care of your emotional and mental health, you will have the ability to address the other questions. Building up your emotional and mental health is the next layer to the foundation of a healthy future for you and the children.

Nursing the Scars

The question I would like to address in this chapter is: "How can I nurse my emotions and scarred heart back to good health?" A broken home leaves more broken pieces than we sometimes care to admit. Apart from the fact that the legal union of a man and woman is broken, individuals walk away with emotional, physical and psychological scars. Probably the most affected individuals are the children from the marriage, but I will deal with that subject separately. In this chapter, I want to focus on the 'me factor': the single mother herself. I will discuss how I went through the healing process myself, and I encourage you to consider different aspects of my healing journey and apply them to yourself as much as possible.

Dealing with Guilt

One of the major issues to deal with is guilt. Many women are familiar with the linc of thought and speech that goes like this:

"It's all my fault... It wouldn't have happened if I had not done so and so... I should not even have married that idiot in the first place ... I have only myself to blame... me ... me ... me!"

Please stop that, right now!!!

If you are spending emotional strength and time feeling guilty, you are doing much more harm than good. In fact, there's no benefit to it whatsoever. This is not to say that you must not assess your past relationship and learn from it. There is however a big difference between one end of the healing spectrum where you learn a lesson and move on, and the other end of the spectrum where you sit down and dwell on the problems, host yourself to a pity party, take a long guilt trip, and cry and cry over spilt milk! You really don't want to spend your energy and time on that!

Your aim should be to recover from the past as quickly as possible. Of course, it's much easier said than done, but I always say that if I went through it with five babies, anyone else can! You can do it! Just believe in the God you serve, and enable yourself to do it. Remember: ***"I can do all things through Christ who gives me strength"*** *(Philippians 4:13)*

The first step however, is to step out of the 'guilt barrel', because all it's going to do is to roll round and round and get you nowhere. One thing to recognize is the popular adage "***it takes two to tango***". It's not *all* your fault! Your spouse had something to do with the breakup too! Again, I'm not encouraging you to push all the blame onto the other party; we need a balanced perspective here.

Bottom-line? It's not all your fault; it's not all his fault. You'll recognize where you failed, and you'll move on; but you must not allow yourself to carry his part of the baggage! That's where many of us make the mistake.

Facing the Facts

In the years following separation, I was so hard on myself. I allowed myself to feel responsible for everything that had gone wrong in my marriage. But then the Lord brought some wonderful brethren my way, who helped me to do the following:

Get out of guilt and into the FACTS,

Allocate blame with balanced reasoning,

Examine ways to improve myself,

Examine ways to MOVE ON!!!

Unknown to me, and long before my marriage eventually ended, I had sunk into depression and denial. I blamed myself for everything that was going wrong: for my spouse's nasty words and for every fight. I mentally accepted that it was "all my fault". Also, my self-esteem had sunk very low. I thought I was really, really ugly! I accepted my spouse's constant put-downs that I was ugly, fat, and a mental moron!

With a Ph.D. in Computer Science, I honestly still wonder how in the world I let that happen, but depression does that to you! I lost sense of who I really was, or where I was heading. I stopped taking care of myself, under the excuse that, "I'm fat and ugly, no one is looking, so why bother?" I also took to compulsive eating, and every time I felt sad, I headed straight for the refrigerator!

In this state of depression, I slowly started to lose environmental awareness, that is, I was generally not aware of where I was sometimes. I did things so mechanically that sometimes when I got to work, I wondered how exactly I got there! Twice I almost got run over because I was 'walking across the green lights'. I just walked across the road and wondered why on earth the drivers were blaring their horns at me! "What in the world is wrong with these hasty people?" I asked in my mind.

Unknown to me, I was mentally slipping away. When I got to work, I would stare at my computer for a long time, and not see anything; I had to exert great effort to concentrate on anything I did, be it work or the children's activities. If I didn't force myself to concentrate, I would easily forget and my mind would slip away into nothing in particular! My boss got worried about me and recommended that I go for counseling. I went to see a Psychologist, but after my first session with him, he told me he thought I was perfectly OK and did not need psychological hclp. Okay? In my mind I disagreed. I sensed that I was not okay, but sometimes it's difficult to argue with a psychologist or most professionals for that matter.

Eventually I came to a point where I had to face the facts: I needed help, and thank God I was not too proud to admit it when I came to the realization of the facts.

Go for Counseling

My sister-in-law, Ebun (God bless her), got so worried about me. She introduced me to Dr. Albert Gyimah, a Consultant Psychiatrist at the Peel Memorial Hospital, Brampton, Ontario. Dr. Gyimah is also a member of All Nations. I hated the idea of seeing a 'psychiatrist'! I told myself I was not mentally ill, so why go see someone who works with 'psychos' and could be a psycho himself? I insisted to Ebun that I had already seen a psychologist, and was in no need whatsoever of a psychiatrist. However, she paid no heed to me, and went ahead and talked to Dr. Gyimah on my behalf. Eventually, I went to see him, not because I wanted to, but because I had to get my loving sister-in-law off my back!

The first time I went to see Dr. Gyimah at the hospital, he simply asked me a few questions, and did a lot of LISTENING. He listened to me talk about myself, about my kids, about life in general, and about my marriage. During that hour, I actually thought the guy was wasting my time! I looked at my watch quite a few times; I wanted to get out of there. As far as I was concerned, all I did was talk, and I could do that anywhere ☺. I was quite an ignorant patient!

Dr. Gyimah is a great listener. He listened, and he took down notes of the things I said. Then based on what he heard, he worked with me to identify the FACTS about my marriage:

that it was a grossly abusive one,

that I had been physically and emotionally beaten up and abused so many times,

that my life had been threatened often,

that I had five very young and insecure children who were in desperate need of a stable and safe environment,

that I was slowly losing my sanity, and

that there was no indication that the situation was going to improve.

At the end of our discussion, Dr. Gyimah gave me some homework. He asked me to go home, think about the ***facts***, and to come up with strategies for handling those facts, and also to draw up all the predicament-resolution options I could think of. He got me thinking about things I had been denying for several years.

The next week, I returned to Dr. Gyimah, and spent another hour looking at different options available to the kids and me. Again I did most of the talking. In fact what we discussed were not really options; they were different 'perspectives' of looking at the only two options I recognized I had: to stay in an abusive marriage in which my children and I could get really hurt, permanently scarred or even killed, or to extricate myself from it. I came up with all kinds of 'reasons' for staying, including:

For the sake of the children

My parents would be so disappointed

What would people say?

It's better to remain married and be a "Mrs." even if we don't communicate in the house…

First, we looked at the option or perspective of staying in my marriage, 'for the sake of the kids'. Dr. Gyimah asked me what long-term effects that would have on the same kids, if the abusive environment remained the same. I thought about that and it was not a pretty picture.

One thing I noticed with Dr. Gyimah's counseling style was that he did not tell me to 'do this', or 'do that'. He gave me information, worked with me to think things through in an informed manner and make my own decisions based on facts, statistics, and other people’s experiences.

Coincidentally at the time I was seeing Dr. Gyimah, there had been a series of suicide-murders involving troubled homes. On that second visit, Dr. Gyimah read me several newspaper excerpts. I particularly remember one: a man in Toronto had killed his wife, three children, and finally himself. I informed Dr. G. that my husband had threatened to take the same course of action: kill me, then the kids, and finally himself, in that order. I was terrified! Just going through those newspaper clips scared the very life out of me!

Secondly, we looked at the option or perspective of staying in my marriage, just to keep up appearances, ‘to look good’ – whatever that means, because I actually didn’t look good (literal meaning) or take good care of myself then. This option meant that I did not want to be counted in the divorce statistics. In other words, I did not want to remove myself from a situation that was slowly but surely destroying my kids and myself simply because I wanted to remain a ‘Mrs. Somebody”, even if the ‘Somebody’ was grossly undeserving.

Then we looked at the perspective of ‘what people and family would say’, and I realized that first, people talk no matter what you do. There are people who will never be satisfied with whatever step you take. Secondly, what good would it make if my parents lost a daughter (me) and 5 grandchildren because that daughter did not take the right decision?

Essentially, Dr. Gyimah made me do a 'cost-benefit' analysis of the two options I had: stay in my marriage, or remove the kids and myself from a negative, harmful, and potentially fatal environment. On the one hand, remaining in the marriage could cost all six of us our lives, and would definitely not help to build up healthy lives or happy children. On the other hand, there would be the difficulties of raising children by myself, but they could end up better because they would have a positive environment to live and grow in... Dr. Gyimah asked me to go home, think about all the facts, and make my own decisions.

I saw Dr. Gyimah twice, for two hours only, but those two hours changed my life. During the months that followed, I read a lot of books about spousal abuse and the behaviors of abusers, what to watch for, how to stay safe, and so on. During those months, I watched my spouse and noticed many things I had previously missed; only now I was more informed and knew what behaviors to watch for. I won't dwell on those details because that's not my intent in this book. However, I finally saw that living in that home, for whatever cover-up reasons, was not the right thing to do.

Basically, the decision was mine, squarely on my laps, and nobody else was going to make it for me, not even my counselor. But I praise the Lord God Almighty for the divine Counselor Himself, the Lord Jesus Christ! We are told in *Isaiah 9:6,*

> ***"For unto us a child is born; unto us a Son is given: and the government shall be upon His shoulder: and His name shall be called Wonderful, Counselor, The***

> ***mighty God, The everlasting Father, The Prince of Peace"***

I went home and prayed and sought the Lord, and He guided me.

It's very important that you go to a competent counselor. They have experience in human psychology and are objective enough to guide you in making the right decisions. When a single woman is on her own, her situation could cloud her sense of judgment and objectivity. It's helpful to speak to a Counselor who has seen other people go through a similar experience. He/she can work with you to overcome your situation. The Bible gives us advice regarding this:

> ***Where no counsel is, the people fall: but in the multitude of counselors there is safety*** *(Proverbs 11:14)*

Staying on your own and trying to plod through the thoughts and confusions of life as a single Mum will not help. You need other people to hold you up and help you stand. We have competent psychologists and psychiatrists who are trained to help, and we must not feel ashamed to seek help. Err on the side of caution if you will, but it's better for a counselor to give you a clean bill of health after the first session (then you're assured that you're okay) than for you to struggle through life without counsel.

Learn Some Lessons From Counselors

Apart from seeing a psychiatrist, I also took advantage of the Community Counseling Services available in the Toronto Municipality. After I fled my home to the Women's Shelter, I talked to some of the Counselors that came to visit us at the shelter. They spent a lot of time with the kids, with my Mum and myself. These professional counselors and social workers helped me recognize the different aspects of my road to recovery.

As far as guilt was concerned, I was able to identify that my guilt stemmed from the fact that I was more worried for my spouse than I was for the rest of us. During counseling however, I recognized that I needed to take care of myself first, so I could be in a better position to take care of my children. They come first, not the spouse; they are delicate, vulnerable, and helpless while he is grown up and can take care of himself! I knew that it was better to protect young and innocent lives than to accommodate an adult spouse who needed emotional and psychiatric help. The counselors helped me to bring it all into proper perspective. Children are so sensitive that one bad move can ruin them for life, and place them in the wrong statistics. I had to be very careful what move I made, because my children were too young to even discern whether my moves were good or not, and that total dependence on me was a great responsibility I knew I must not shirk.

Through counseling I recognized that since it takes two to make a really nasty marriage, one party must not take all the blame in a depressed state of mind. If that happens, the other party would feel *justified* in what is going on, and may actually be encouraged to continue the abusive behavior. I discovered that my taking all the blame was partly responsible for the continuance of abuse in my home.

As a single Mum, you need to look at some of the above psychological facts, and to understand where you have failed in your relationship. However, the aim is not to beat you up or put you down, but to help you determine your weak areas and to identify areas you need to improve for the future. You need to speak to counselors and social workers who are professionally trained to work with you to identify these facts and directions. Again, it's quite difficult to identify these loopholes by yourself. Part of taking care of the 'me-factor' is to create a proper foundation upon which you can lay the other topics we will discuss in this book. Getting a proper mental and psychological state through counseling is key to that foundation.

Cultivate a Confidant Relationship

Apart from Psychologists and Counselors, it's important to have a personal confidant whom you can discuss with at any time. Of course God is our best confidant, and I encourage you to pray and talk to God about everything that bothers you. He cares deeply about every thing that concerns you, to the point of knowing the number of hairs of your head! ***(Matthew 10:30)***

At the same time, God encourages us to find solace and wisdom in sharing our concerns with one another, and to seek counsel, for in the multitude of counselors there is safety. Also, friendship is good because "a friend loves at all times" ***(Proverbs 17:17*)**. Moreover,

> ***Iron sharpens iron; so a man sharpens the countenance of his friend*** *(Proverbs 27:17)*.

There are many times when it's not convenient or even appropriate to talk to a Counselor. For one, they don't come cheap; you pay fees to see them. Secondly, there are some very seemingly simple decision-making processes that you really don't need to work out with professional help. Thirdly, you do have to book an appointment to see them. They are not available 24x7, and you may have some pressing questions that must be answered in the nick of time, or else it's useless to talk to anyone about them. Lastly, every girl has a right to cry sometimes, and especially for a single Mom, you need a shoulder to cry on, maybe not always in the literal sense, but in many ways you need someone who is available when you really want to vent or complain!

In cases like these, you need a friend, a confidant. I thank God for my friends Isaac and Angel Obo-Rockson. Isaac is my confidant and prayer-partner, a good brother in All Nations, who has designated himself my *personal shrink* so to say. He's always there to listen to my complaints, and 'whining'. And of course when I'm off track, like when I say all kinds of negative things about the male Homo sapiens, he calls me to order. He's not afraid to tell me when I've missed it

It's important to cultivate a confidant relationship, not with just anyone, but with someone who can truly keep your secrets and respect your vulnerabilities, not someone who will act as a *broadcast station* and tell the whole world what it is you're struggling with. Your confidant could be of your gender or someone of the opposite gender. What matters is that your relationship is clearly a confidant relationship and nothing more, especially if he or she is married. For example, Isaac is married, so we have lots of boundaries that my discussions with him do not cross, and in many cases, I give him permission to discuss some things with Angel, so their relationship is not in any way jeopardized.

A confidant relationship is truly therapeutic, because it enables you to talk about problems at any time, and your confidant can pray with you. Indeed where two or three are gathered in God's name, He is there to answer their prayers, and a confidant relationship is definitely included in this divine plan for God's children.

Chapter 5. You Are Beautiful! Don't Let Anyone Convince You Otherwise!

> ***... Thou art beautiful, O my love, as Tirzah ... turn away thine eyes from me, for they have overcome me; thy hair is as a flock of goats that appear from Gilead. Thy teeth are as a flock of sheep which go up from the washing, whereof everyone bears twins, and there is none barren among them. As a piece of a pomegranate, are thy temples within thy locks. There are threescore queens, and four score concubines, and virgins without number. My dove, my undefiled is but one; she is the only one of her mother ... how beautiful are thy feet with shoes, O prince's daughter! The joints of thy thighs are like jewels, the work of the hands of a cunning workman. Thy navel is like a round goblet which wants not liquor; thy belly is like a heap of wheat set about with lilies. Thy two breasts are like two young roes that are twins. Thy neck is like a tower of ivory; thy eyes like the fish-pools in Heshbon ... thy nose is as the tower of Lebanon... Thy head upon thee is like Carmel, and the hair of thy head like purple; the king is held in the galleries. How fair and how pleasant art thou, O love, for delights!*** *(Song of Solomon 6:1 – 7:13)*

The above quote is a beautiful rendition from the Bible itself, signifying the beautiful love between a man and a woman, in this case, Solomon and his 'beloved'. They were madly in love, as we will put it today. They said lots of sweet nothings to each other. "Your eyes are like this, ..., your toes are like that..." Amazing how true this is for many of us, when we were dating the men we married. Do you remember? He practically worshipped the ground you stepped on. You were the "sunshine of his day, the sugar in his tea, the salt in soup". If he didn't hear your voice he would lose his appetite, and so on and so forth. Basically, you were the most beautiful thing that ever happened to him, and the most beautiful girl he ever knew!

So what happened? Without going to the negative side, my question to you in this chapter is: if you were "the most beautiful girl in the world then", what makes you think you are still not the most beautiful girl in the world now? Of course you must know that you were, and still are beautiful. So why is it that when he stopped believing that you are beautiful, you also allowed yourself to believe the same lie?

My challenge to you is this: do not base your feelings about yourself on the feelings of someone else? Maybe your spouse stopped believing that you are beautiful – that does not cancel the fact that you are still beautiful! You were beautiful when you got married; you are still beautiful; and you will stay beautiful till the day you die! Better believe it!

They say, "Beauty is in the eye of the beholder". Maybe you depended on your spouse to do the beholding. But now that he's not there anymore, the 'beholder' has to change: the new beholder must be you, and what you must see of yourself is "Still Beautiful"! It all depends on how you see yourself.

How do you see yourself?

One of the building blocks for the psychological wholeness of any woman is how she *sees* herself, her perception of how *others* see her, and consequently how she *feels* about herself. As we introduced in the last chapter, we must love ourselves before we can love anyone else around us, including our children.

However, many women do not feel very good about themselves; neither do we all accept ourselves as we are. Those who are skinny may want to put on a little extra weight; those who are chubby like me may want to lose some weight; those who are really tall wish they were a little shorter; and the list goes on. The end result becomes a host of unsatisfied women, including myself, who just question our Maker for making us the way we are!

Apart from the dissatisfaction that comes from within, people are susceptible to the comments and reactions of others. Even starting from elementary school age, my 'friends' could tease me about how fat I am, and I could let that torment me for a long time! To make matters much worse, this does not end with elementary school; even in marriage and other adult relationships, we constantly hear negative comments that affect the way we feel about ourselves. These comments are like little drops of water out of a rock, but eventually, they bore a large enough hole in our minds, a hole that tells us that we are not beautiful, that we are not good, and so on and so forth!

Does this relate with you? What can we do about our personal perception of our beauty or our goodness? What can we do about the psychological holes that have been drilled into our subconscious by the things said by friends, relatives, and especially spouses? In this chapter I discuss my long road to feeling better about myself, and the beautiful people that God brought my way to help me on that journey to a higher sense of self-worth.

Deal with Low Self-Esteem

One of the major problems I had was very low self-esteem, which got worse and worse with years of mental and psychological abuse in my marriage. Take for example, if I had an employee whom I told over and over again that he's 'no good', it is highly possible that he would, deliberately or subconsciously, give up on his productivity, probably to spite me in a 'So what? Go to hell' manner, or in actual direct emotional response to my calling him a 'no-good'.

If one gets called a 'shapeless amoeba' frequently enough, in and out of pregnancies, words like these sink so deep into the subconscious, and eat so strong into the mind, that one tends to believe them after some time. And the dangerous thing is that the person now begins to behave in a way to promote the negative thoughts, and to bring them into physical manifestation. It ends up being a cycle of low self-esteem, and it takes only the power of God to deliver someone from that devil!

I have been pregnant 5 times for my five beautiful children (God bless my children; I won't trade them for anything!). When I got married, I was tall and skinny, weighing about 120lbs, which was quite underweight for my 5foot-8-height, but I was quite slim. After just my first pregnancy, I gained about 70lbs! I went from the tall and skinny girl to a really chubby me! I know; pregnancy does that to you. And of course, with each subsequent pregnancy, I put on a few more pounds, and did not lose any! To make matters a little bit more complicated, my kids are all close in age: I had Jerry in 1992, Peace in 1993, Emmanuel in 1994, Faith in 1995, and Gabby in early 1997. Averaging one year apart, five kids in rapid succession doesn't give anyone any chance to recover physically. By the time I had my last child, I had gone from 120lbs to 200lbs! Even *I* knew I had a real challenge to deal with!

Rather than give me positive encouragement to lose weight, my spouse resorted to name-calling and mental abuse. I got called all kinds of names, from 'fat pig' to 'shapeless amoeba'! I heard those names so many times that I actually let them sink into my subconscious, to the point that I gave up and didn't even try to lose weight or look good at all. After all, I was supposed to be shapeless! My self-esteem was at a terrible low! I had to deal with that.

For me, I had trouble with my weight and appearance. Other women have trouble with other areas of their bodies, like their hair, bust only, butts only, anything! Now, I'm not suggesting that you must go and lose weight. Rather, I am suggesting that you deal with whatever poses a problem for you, or aggravates low self-esteem in your life. For me, weight was the problem. For you, it could be different.

The main crux of the matter here is that you must deal with the issues that make you feel bad about yourself and issues that keep your self-esteem at a low point. These are issues that make a woman not to love herself as an individual, or to feel uncomfortable in the presence of others. For me, I didn't feel good about myself because I did not like what I saw in the mirror, and I lived in an environment where I had no motivation or encouragement to do something about it. Once I left my abusive home, I needed to deal with low self-esteem, and I thank God for the people He brought my way to help me.

Using my beloved Christian community, the Lord showed me that low self-esteem is actually an evil spirit. It works by taking our attention from who we are in Christ, to who people see us as. I learned to recognize that the Lord God has made me beautiful; and the fact that my spouse did not see me that way is really ***not*** my problem, but rather his!

I thank God for the life of my Senior Pastor's wife, Rev. Rose Donkor, popularly and lovingly known as "Mama Rose". One Sunday morning on my way to the church sanctuary, I dropped by the church office for something I don't remember at this time. Mama Rose looked at me, smiled, held me by the hand and took me into her office. She took her hairbrush out of her handbag and brushed my hair. She took some of her makeup powder and lipstick and put them on me. Then she picked up her mirror and said to me, "Look! You are a very beautiful woman. You must begin to take better care of yourself, you know".

I was so touched I almost cried! Mama Rose demonstrated the love of Christ and the care of a mother by taking me aside and spending a few minutes to show me what I was supposed to know, which the devil had kept me from doing because of low self-esteem. She called me into her office a few more times after that, just to check that I was doing what she had instructed me to do. Later, she handed me over to a hairdresser in the church, and asked her to 'work' on my hair.

I recently attended an All Nations "Encounter" program, in which I was challenged to 'encounter myself' and the devil's attempt to put me down. During that conference, we were reminded of David's words in Psalm 139:14-16:

> ***"I will praise Thee, for I am fearfully and wonderfully made; marvelous are Thy works; and that my soul knoweth right well. My substance was not hid from Thee, when I was made in secret, and curiously wrought in the lowest parts of the earth. Thy eyes did see my substance, yet being unperfect; and in Thy book all my members were written, which in continuance were fashioned, when as yet there was none of them."***

As a woman you need to recognize that the Lord God spent time to *fashion* you in a curious (amazing), and wonderful way. In the whole wide world, there is no one like you! Even if you have an identical twin, the technological advances of today in the areas of biometric recognition attest to the fact that your twin does not have identical differentiating features as you! You have different fingerprints, different eyes, preferences, gait, voice pattern, and other distinguishing features, than anyone else in God's amazing creation. So, if God has spent time to make you so wonderfully, you must feel special about yourself no matter what the devil or a hateful spouse says about it!!!

When you recognize who you are in God, and spend time uprooting the lies of haters from your mind, your self-esteem has no choice but to shoot all the way up to the sky!

Learn to Assert Yourself!

One other problem I had was not being assertive. This goes hand in hand with low self-esteem. On an assertiveness spectrum, there are those who cannot assert themselves in any situation and consequently have to deal with very low self-esteem. At the other end of the spectrum are people who over-assert themselves, and are aggressive as a result. These people also have low self-esteem but exhibit it via aggressiveness. Somewhere in the middle is the group of people who can assert themselves, are not aggressive, but relate with people around them in a balanced manner.

Most aggressive people exhibit controlling tendencies. They work by intimidating their targets or victims into submitting to their aggressive control. Some ways that aggressive and controlling husbands work include name-calling, and physical battery. In most cases, their victims are at the opposite end of the spectrum, and cannot assert themselves enough to get the controlling bully off their backs! Such was the case in my marriage. I was heavily intimidated and controlled and couldn't fight back in any positive way. I really had a big problem. For example, if we went out shopping for clothes, although I liked bright colors, my spouse preferred me to wear dark colors, and many times I would take the dark colors even though I didn't want them!

After separation, I knew I had to learn to assert myself. I started from the public library, and was quite pleasantly surprised to discover that they had lots of books and tapes on assertiveness. I borrowed some tape series and listened to them over and over again. I began to learn to say 'no' when I really meant to say 'no'. I slowly deduced that the problem with unassertive individuals is that they are trying to please the other person at their own expense and to their detriment!

Then I began to look at unassertiveness from a Biblical perspective. There are two major forces at work in an unassertive person:

Fear

Lying

When a child is confronted by a bully, that child almost always gives in as a result of fear – fear that the bully would hurt him or her. This is the same scenario for adults, but as adults, we should know better, right? Wrong! Even as grown ups, many of us still allow ourselves to live in fear in certain relationships. An instance is the mafia, where gang members are simply terrified of their boss, and would do anything just to be in his good books. A simpler case of course is where, for cultural or other reasons, a wife is so terrified of her husband that the couple lives in a master-slave relationship. Unfortunately, when you live in fear and the bully spouse sees it, he becomes more and more aggressive and controlling, and you become more and more fearful!

However, the Bible tells me that as a child of God, I must not fear, not my spouse, not the mad man on the street, not even the devil himself:

> ***For God hath not given us the spirit of fear, but of power, and of love, and of a sound mind*** *(II Timothy 2:7)*

> ***What shall we then say to these things? If God be for us, who can be against us? He that spared not His own Son, but delivered Him up for us all, how shall He not with Him also freely give us all things?*** *(Romans 8: 31, 32)*

> ***No weapon that is fashioned against you shall prosper, and every tongue that shall rise against you, you shall condemn. This is the heritage of the servants of the Lord, and their righteousness is of me, says the Lord.*** *(Isaiah 54:17)*

There are many, many scriptures that tell me that I have been given authority and boldness and power over the devil himself, so why in the world should I be afraid of a spouse?

When the Lord deals with the spirit of fear in your life, unassertiveness will fly away. The fear to say "No" to your spouse, or in fact, anyone around you, will begin to express itself in a bolder, more expressive way like,

"No thanks, I'd rather have the pink one. I really

don't like black!" Or,

"You know what? I know we really need to discuss this. I feel strongly that we must not sweep this subject under the carpet any longer!" Or,

"No, I don't like it when you yell or scream at me like that, and I want you to stop doing that".

Or say to your boss, "No, I'd rather not work this weekend. I have other plans with my family".

If you have been unassertive, you need to begin to learn how to express yourself clearly and firmly to people around you, especially your children. As a single mother, this is particularly important for your children. I'll discuss this when I focus on the children.

The second root of unassertiveness is lying. Most of the time however, the root of lying is fear, unless someone is a habitual liar. So if you deal with fear, lying *normally* tends to go away. Unfortunately, there are still some who find themselves in an unassertive position and lie, not out of fear, but again just not to offend the other person.

When I look at the Holy Scriptures on the subject of lying, I discover that all lying is simply lying, and there's nothing like a small white lie or a big colored one! This vital issue was also addressed by Rev. Veronica Adu-Bobie at the All Nations Encounter Weekend I attended very recently.

As the Bible says in Revelation 21:8:

> ***"But the fearful and unbelieving, and the abominable, and murderers and whoremongers, and sorcerers and idolaters and all liars, shall have their part in the lake which burns with fire and brimstone; which is the second death."***

We see then that liars are counted as guilty as a murderer, a witch, and people who commit abominable crimes! So why would you want to go to hell by remaining in unassertiveness and lying?

When I was a little girl in elementary school, we used to sing a song that goes like this:

Wherever you go

Wherever you be

Do not say 'yes'
When you mean to say 'no'!

This is the crux of unassertiveness: saying 'yes' (or 'no') when you mean to say 'no' (or 'yes'). I pray that the Lord will deliver us from unassertiveness, and help us to be free to express ourselves in all our relationships.

Change Your Dominant Thoughts: Think and Speak the Scriptures, not Negatives

I was blessed to meet a beloved brother, George, who

taught me that a person always acts to establish his dominant thoughts, whether positive or negative. This is very much in line with Jesus' admonition in Matthew 15:18-20:

> ***"But those things which proceed out of the mouth come forth from the heart; and they defile the man. For out of the heart proceed evil thoughts, murders, adulteries, fornications, thefts, false witness, blasphemies; these are the things which defile a man, but to eat with unwashed hands does not defile a man"***

Also, King Solomon warns in Proverbs 4:23,

> ***"Keep your heart with all diligence, for out of it are the issues of life".***

King Solomon brings the above proverb into much louder-ringing clarity when he says in Proverbs 18:21, that:

> ***" … death and life are in the power of the tongue …!"***

When I began to meditate on Proverbs 18:21, I was shocked at how much we destroy our own selves by the things we say! However, the things we say are very strongly connected to the things we allow to enter into, ***and settle in***, our minds!

What we allow to *settle* in our minds is what we act out, whether we like our thoughts or not. It's one thing for a thought to flash across your mind and you ignore it; it has no lasting effect on your thinking, beliefs, or personality. However, if we entertain that flashing thought, and stop to think and talk about it, it would eventually affect our minds and our behavior, whether we want it to or not!

Even if I don't like to think of myself as a 'shapeless amoeba' or a 'fat pig', if I allow those thoughts to eat into my mind, I would begin to eat like a 'fat pig' and to look and dress like a 'shapeless amoeba'!

Although my counselors had helped me to identify my low self-esteem, I could not bring myself to fight its historical grip effectively. The motivating tapes I had listened to had helped me to learn how to better assert myself in different situations, but I still struggled with the thoughts that had been internalized in my mind for so many years. It was a battle that had to be won and I was not sure how to go about it.

I met George in December 1999, and noticed right away that he was quite a scripture-thinker and scripture-speaker, and he spoke the word of God to his situations very promptly. When George was sick, rather than say 'I am sick', he said, "I am healed in Jesus' Name. ***By His stripes I am healed***"! (I Peter 2:24) When George was broke, he would not say, "Oh dear, I am so broke it's not funny", he would say, "***The Lord shall supply all my need according to His riches in glory by Christ Jesus***"! (Philippians 4:19). I was so impressed!

In the same manner I noticed George's positive Christian attitude to life, he also noticed that I put myself down and didn't say anything positive or good about myself. One day George remarked that I looked pretty in a new outfit I was wearing and my reply was something in this line: "Oh no! I'm not pretty at all; I'm just covering up this big old fat body!" George was so alarmed, he said to me, "Don't you ever speak of yourself like that!" Then he proceeded to give me a really loooonnng (arghh!!!) lecture about how I am made in the image of God Himself, I am the temple of the Holy Spirit, and the beauty of God is upon me, and so on. I was so grateful to God when George finished with that lecture, but I learnt something eventually from my dealings with him – that I must speak positively about myself and about every situation in which I find myself.

George made me do a few simple self-esteem-building exercises. The most impacting of these was standing in front of my mirror and making positive statements to my image in the mirror. So on many occasions, I would stand at my mirror and literally use words on myself from head to toe like this:

> ***"I am beautiful. The Lord has given me great hair, good skin, a good face, lovely eyes, well-lined lips, good shoulders, beautifully full breasts, lovely hands and fingers, good hips, great legs, great back-side, and size-8.5 feet!" "I am beautiful. The Lord has given me beauty for ashes; I must take off the ashes and polish the beauty"...*** *and so on and so forth.*

It was quite difficult at first. When I said, "I am beautiful," my mind would retort with "look who's kidding herself!" Of course, my mind had it registered that "I am fat and ugly", so it took me several months of genuine attempts to actually get myself to say, "I am beautiful" with good confidence. It was a practical battle, but George was persistent. He made me do it and slowly I began to feel good about myself.

That is however only the first step. Feeling *good* about yourself is ***not*** the same as feeling *satisfied* with who you are. If you feel *good* about yourself, you obey the Lord's command to 'love your neighbor as yourself…", since you've got to love yourself first in order to extend that love to your neighbor, signifying others around you. The next step will be to find ways of improving and polishing yourself, to make yourself better, as again commanded by the word of God. I'll address this second part of the equation in the next three chapters.

In the same way, I used the word of God on my finances, my health, my children's behavior, and other things I encounter everyday. I began to make confessions like "The Lord will prosper all that I lay my hands upon to do", "As long as I pay all my tithes and bring all the tithes into the Lord's house, the Lord has rebuked the devourer for my sake", and so on.

You must realize that you have great promises buried in the word of God; you need to dig them out as gold, and apply them through the things you say, to your life's situations. II Peter 1: 2-4 tells us:

> ***"Grace and peace be multiplied to you through the knowledge of God, and of Jesus our Lord, according as His divine power, has given unto us, all things that pertain to life and godliness, through the knowledge of him that has called us to glory and virtue, whereby are given unto us exceeding great and precious promises: that by these we might be partakers of the divine nature, having escaped the corruption that is in the world through lust."***

The Lord has given us, through His word, all things that pertain to life and godliness. He has made provisions for us but we need to tap into them. That tapping starts with our confessions or the things we allow ourselves to say into or from our spirits.

Begin to confess the word of God today and watch the changes begin to come. It's simply amazing! When you dwell on positive confessions based on the word of God, several things happen:

You'll feel better

You'll experience an uplifting and encouragement in your spirit and you'll receive more strength to go on

Most importantly, you'll effectively begin to call those things that are not as though they were, and bring them to materialization from the spiritual plane of your pronouncements to the physical.

Notice in Romans 4:17, that Abraham received the promise of God that he would have a son, and although he was an old man and Sarah his wife was way past child-bearing age, Abraham hoped against hope, because he believed in ***" … God who quickens the dead, and calls those things which be not as though they were."***

It's quite an amazing phenomenon and I encourage you to study the Bible, the word of God, and begin to speak His promises to your situation. Begin to call into existence, those things you want to happen in your life. God has given us thousands of promises in His word. We only suffer and perish because we are ignorant of those promises and consequently we cannot apply them to our lives. You don't have to suffer like many do. Dig into the word and speak to your mountains! They will move, in Jesus' Name!

Chapter 6. Fulfill Your Dreams – My Personal Pickup / Progress (3P) Challenge

In this chapter, I want to build on the foundations I've laid in previous chapters, to focus on ways a single mother can ***improve*** herself, and not allow herself to settle for the status quo.

One of the things I discovered when my children and I were in a Women's Shelter for two months was the kind of mental attitude in most of the single women I met there. Many of them had completely given up! They ***seemed*** to want to remain in the situations they were in. For most of them, as long as they received regular cheques from the government everything was alright. During my discussions with several of these women however, I discovered that they had lots and lots of potential and talents! They were very intelligent and gifted women with great dreams, but for some reasons, they had given up their dreams. Quite heartbreaking, but in the years following that experience, I have seen the same phenomenon again and again in many single mothers I've met.

Why is this so? We have discussed some of the reasons already. Every single mother needs counseling. Every single mother needs to love herself. We all need to find a community to belong to. We all need to address problems with self-esteem and assertiveness. These are all part of the foundation we lay for a better, stronger future.

However, once we've cleaned up, we need to BUILD up the woman we always wanted to be, and improve upon her. We need to begin to work on our dreams and on fulfilling them! *This is the most challenging but rewarding part of being a successful single mother.* This is where the Lord Jesus Christ has helped me to succeed, and when people ask me, "Rose, how in the world do you do it?" I point them to the Rock, the Lord Jesus Christ, who has given me the strength and persistence to stick to my dreams. We all need dreams, for without a dream, there is no drive for life.

What Are Your Dreams?

The question I'd like you to start with in this chapter is: what are your dreams? Think back ... way back to when you were a little girl. Think about when you played house and games with your girlfriends, when you wrote essays in elementary school about 'When I Grow Up"... Think... What were your aspirations? Those are the things that you wanted to be when you were a kid. Did you know that a child's aspirations go with that kid even through adulthood? Did you know that if your childhood dreams and aspirations are not fulfilled, you could go through life as a completely unsatisfied adult? For many people that is the case.

In this chapter, I want to challenge you to shoot for

self-fulfillment and go for your dreams.

Unfortunately, things do go wrong as they sometimes do. Many people therefore give up as if that's the end of the world. But I have really good news for you: ***It doesn't have to be so; don't give up; you can still make it!*** The fact that your marriage relationship ended does not mean you have to bury all your dreams along with it. If you buried your childhood aspirations and dreams with your relationship, please go and dig them back up! Exhume them! You can still achieve your dreams. It's not an easy task, but with the Lord's help, you can succeed. It is possible!

My Personal Pickup / Progress Challenge

Now let's do an exercise that I have dubbed my 'Personal Pickup / Progress (3P) Challenge'. The name of this challenge is quite deliberate.

First, it's a *Pickup Challenge* because I must challenge myself to pick up the broken pieces of my life, rather than sit down and cry over spilt milk.

Secondly, it's a *Personal Challenge* because the pickup must be done by me, not by anyone else. I must not allow myself to fall into the entrapment of shifting the responsibility for *my* life to somebody else. Also, although I have been hurt by people who once loved me, I cannot afford to sit down and wait for them to fix my life for me, because they never will! They want me to stay down! So I must strive to pick *myself* up, because no one else will do it for me.

Thirdly, it's a *Progress Challenge* because my focus is on *improving* myself, and making progress. I must not allow myself to stay in the status quo, or to remain mediocre. I must challenge myself to be better than I was yesterday, and my focus is on finding ways of improving myself on a daily basis.

This is an exercise that I have done hundreds of times already. I've found it most rewarding, and I'm sure it will benefit you. As you read, I'd like you to join me actively, so we can do it together. The challenge consists of 6 pages:

Destination Page

Interrupt Page

Excuses Page

Rework Page

Working Page

Medals Page

Destination: Please take a notebook, and on a fresh page, write down all your childhood dreams. If you don't recall your childhood aspirations, write down the things you always wanted to be from as far back as you can remember, till the present. This is your ***Destination Page.***

I like to look at the attainment of our dreams as a journey through life. We embark on the journey from childhood, and our destinations are the aspirations we always had, like wanting to be a doctor, an engineer, a lawyer, and so on.

Interrupt: Flip to a fresh page and write down your disappointments with yourself – where you think you have failed. This is your ***Interrupt Page.*** I like to look at the disappointments in our lives, not as failures, but as ***temporary interruptions*** to our ultimate targets or destinations. The reason many people give up is because they see disappointments as failures, and so they close the chapter and that's the end of their journey through life. If you consider problems rather as temporary interruptions, you can address those disappointments and mistakes and resolve them more effectively.

For each of these disappointments, ask yourself which ones can ***stop*** you from achieving your goal (showstoppers), which ones have high to medium impact on your possible success, and which have little impact. The high-impact ones are the ones without which you cannot progress to fulfilling your dreams.

Put a dot beside all the ones you think will have little impact on the possibility of achieving your dreams. Make a note to yourself to clean up the low-impact interrupts quickly. We'll revisit them in the ***Working Page.***

Put a star beside all the ones you think might have a big impact. For example, if you wanted to be a teacher and for some reason you quit high school, that would have a big impact.

Rework: Flip to another page and re-list your high-impact disappointments (the ones with the stars on your ***Interrupt Page***). For each one, write down how you think you can overcome them. What are the things you need to do to jump the hurdles presented by these high-impact showstoppers? For example, if you had quit high school, write, "Get a high school diploma". Call this page your ***Rework Page.*** Spend a lot of time on this page, because the degree to which you succeed in fulfilling your dreams will be impacted by how honest and thorough you are with identifying the areas you need to rework. The homework you have to do is on your Rework Page. I prefer not to call this any other name like 'repair page' or 'homework page', because the challenge before us is much more complex than 'homework' suggests, and 'repair' sounds like something is really damaged and I don't like to think of working to fulfill my dreams as a repair exercise. I like to look at this concept as a rework because it suggests that I had done some work before (even though it might have been negative), and I'll like to work again to improve upon my previous inefficient work. It sounds more satisfying from a rework perspective.

Excuses: Next, flip to a new page and call this your ***Excuses Page***. On this page, write all the excuses you have given yourself to *not* move forward on your dreams. I'll give you a hint. For example, many decades ago, people thought that engineering or medicine were meant for men only, and so only very few women ventured into the engineering or medical domains. However, things have changed and we see more and more women engineers and doctors. For some of our pioneering female engineers and doctors, a typical excuse to not attempt it must have been "Oh, but I'm a woman". Other excuses could include "I don't have the money", "I'm too old", and so on. These excuses are the things that stop people short in their dream tracks, and combined with the next page, my plan is usually to attack my excuses. I like to see my excuses as my own mountain, and with the help of God, I work to overcome and pull them down!

Working: Next, flip to a new page and prioritize the items on your Rework Page. Identify the ones that have to be done before others, and which ones are more urgent than the others. Prioritize them from 1 to 100, 1000, [however many they are]. For some people, it might be 5 things, for others it might be 50 things. Just prioritize them according to their urgency, ordering constraints, and perceived importance. Women are good at this: we make up shopping lists and recipes all the time. Call this your ***Working Page***. I like to look at this as 'working memory', or some agenda, which you will address one item at a time.

In a separate section of your Working Page, place all the low-impact interrupts you identified on your ***Interrupt Page***. Assign them Priority 0. Although they have low impact, I find that the 'little things' could constitute a stumbling block sometimes, if left unchecked. You may wish to sift out those you wish to ignore if you think they won't have any impact whatsoever on your progress, but address and clean them up as soon as possible, to make way and reserve energy for the bigger things to come.

Medals: Lastly, flip to a new page, and label it the ***Medals Page***. This is where you'll record your successes as you reach them. If you work with me on this Challenge successfully, you will, over the next few weeks, months and years, slowly but surely move items from the Working Page to the Medals Page. I call this the Medals Page because every interrupt you overcome is a great achievement. You should give yourself a big pat on the back, and reward yourself with a medal for each victory! Moreover, when you move an item to the Medals Page, you get an indication of getting closer and closer to your Destination Page.

So the challenge you have before you is to attempt to fill in the gap between your Destination Page and your Interrupt Page. You can achieve this by the areas you identify on your Rework Page.

Using the Personal Pickup / Progress Challenge

I've found my 3P Challenge very useful for both short-term and long-term goals. For example, when I lived in the Women's Shelter, one of the items that moved very quickly to top priority in my Working Page was to find an apartment, or buy a home, no matter how small or cheap, to get us out of the shelter as quickly as possible. I frantically called my realtor, Nnamdi Anurukem, and with his help I was able to purchase and move into a small condominium one month later! One of the biggest obstacles I had was coming up with a down-payment, but Nnamdi and I overcame that. It was constant juggling between my Working Page and my Medals Page, and eventually, getting a home moved into the Medals Page!

For long-term goals, I added my desire to write a book. It took me several years before I settled down to writing my first book, The Video Game (a children's book in my *Happy Gang* series), but I did it! So you see that the Personal Pickup / Progress Challenge can work for you for all kinds of targets.

Sometimes it's quite helpful to put short-term goals in your Working Page, because when you achieve those short-term goals, the joy and elation you feel will give you the motivation and new adrenalin to continue with the long-term goals. This is the importance of placing all your low-impact items as priority 0. However, please do not allow the low-impact items to distract your focus from the high-impact ones. For me I find that it's easier to multi-task and do them side-by-side, by spending a little time each day on my low-impact items, and a little time on the high-impact ones as well. Multi-tasking is one thing that women do very easily, and I'm sure you will find that you can achieve different items concurrently, just the way you sometimes make phone calls and cook and clean all at the same time!

You must also be careful not to feel discouraged with the slowness of achieving longer-term goals. Remember that Rome was not built in a day. These things take time, and you need to pray to the Lord everyday for the strength and determination to pull through.

Group discussions are excellent for working on this challenge, because a group of women can come up with excellent ideas about what needs to be improved in their personal lives, and they can all chip in strategies for achieving these goals.

Bottom line, you need to embark on a self-improving progress project. Make a dress, learn to sew, write a book, draw a picture, go to school, go for a competition, whatever! Get busy, and challenge yourself!

Why You Need To Challenge Yourself

Why bother with this challenge? I'll give you the biggest reason that motivated me: so that when my ex-husband sees me in the future, he would be ashamed of himself for treating me badly! Sounds funny? Why not? A girl is entitled to some fun, you know! I was actually amused at God's own humor sometimes. Many of us read Psalms 23, and quote it inside out. Think about this verse:

> ***You set a table before me in the presence of my enemies; you anoint my head with oil, my cup runs over***

Do you realize how much God wants to set a table of prosperity in front of you, and in the presence or sight of your enemies? God wants those who hated you in the past to be amazed in envy, when they see what the Lord has done for you. He wants your cup to run over with success, but He cannot do it if you just sit back and fold your hands.

More importantly, succeed for your own joy's sake. You've got to feel confident and walk with your head held high. This kind of confidence comes only when you have slowly but surely overcome your stumbling blocks and come out on top!

Lastly, you need to challenge yourself to improve, for your children's sakes. Can you possibly imagine the pride in your children when they say to their friends, "Mum is graduating from College", or "Mum has a job! No more food bank!", or "Mum's going to be a lawyer!" They would beam with pride, knowing that they have a hardworking, well-accomplished Mum! Also, you lay a good foundation for them, a good pattern to follow, knowing that they cannot give up on themselves, but must work with God's help to overcome and succeed in life.

Challenge yourself! It's worth it many times over!

Things Not to Put in the Personal Pickup / Progress Challenge

It's important to use the 3P Challenge for things that will benefit and improve you, not things that will cause aggravation or annoyance.

For example, I've worked with some women who want to settle scores with their ex-husbands or their mothers-in-law, or other relationships. For one thing, settling a score is not your destination. Your destination is to improve yourself to such an extent that you will be more fulfilled and satisfied in life, and feel good about yourself. I'll address settling scores in Chapter 11, but for now, please focus the Personal Pickup / Progress Challenge on improving *yourself* and not on wasting your emotions or energy on non-beneficial relationships.

So you may need to re-examine your Rework and Working Pages, and strike out items that will not be of any benefit to you.

In the next chapter, I'll address some areas I have focused on myself, and which I perceive a lot of single mothers need to focus on themselves.

Chapter 7. Shoot for Financial Freedom

Part of the challenge of being a single mother is the financial responsibility of taking care of yourself and the children, especially if they have a dead-beat father who won't contribute to their upbringing. However, in order to be financially buoyant, you need a good education and a good financial strategy. Secondly, as I pointed out in Chapter 5, we all need to take good care of ourselves, not just for the kids' sakes, but also for our own happiness.

In this chapter, I address some of the items you need to add to your ***Working Page*** as discussed in the last chapter. Focusing on gaining financial freedom can revolutionize your life. You will go through the rest of your life knowing that you don't have to struggle anymore.

First, Recognize This: Welfare Hurts Your Self-Esteem!

Several developed countries provide a welfare system where they give out portions of taxpayers' taxes to the underprivileged, the homeless, single mothers, and so on. I personally laud the welfare program; it is a really good way to ensure that citizens are well catered for, especially those who truly cannot help themselves.

This is a sensitive subject, and I have chosen my words quite carefully in my statement above. You'll notice that I support use of the welfare system for people who *truly cannot help themselves.*

There are some valid reasons why an able-bodied, mentally sound single mother would collect welfare checks as opposed to working. One common reason I've come across is the fact that sometimes paid income is not as high as the welfare check. This does make sense until you look at the big picture I'm trying to paint in this book – that you can overcome this huge hurdle and move way beyond the welfare check! In this chapter, I'll show you how.

We must recognize that if somebody can work and help herself, and still collects welfare, it's most likely because she doesn't realize that she is actually hurting herself!

First, welfare is really not good for your self-esteem. If I collect free money that I don't work for, I would have no sense of *accomplishment* in getting that money, and I lose the psychological satisfaction I could get from knowing that I've received a *reward* for something I've done, like work. Without a sense of accomplishment when you receive that monthly free check, you *slowly but surely* erode on your own self-esteem.

Secondly, welfare encourages people to be lazy and idle, and to consequently get into mischief. Laziness is a violation of spiritual laws, for indeed anyone who does not work must not eat, according to the word of God:

> ***For even when we were with you, this we commanded you, that if any would not work, neither should he eat.*** *(II Thessalonians 3:10)*

When anyone is lazy and does not work, the person becomes an easy candidate for boredom and idleness, which leads to trouble and unbeneficial associations. When this happens, if you're sincere with yourself, you don't feel good.

In order for you as a single mother to truly feel good about yourself, you must lay an example of hard work for your children, and welfare is not a good example: children learn from what they see, and if they see that you stay home, do nothing, and collect free money that you have not worked for, guess what they'll do in the future – the same thing or even worse! Like mother like daughters and sons …

If you are able-bodied, sound-minded, and are currently collecting free welfare checks, please put a *high-impact* item on your ***Working Page*** to slowly extricate yourself from it. You need to feel good about yourself; you need a clear sense of accomplishment. You need to retrain and empower yourself as we'll discuss in this chapter. And you need to rise beyond the miserly welfare checks and project yourself to higher success! You can do it, and I say, "Go for it, girl!"

Attack the Root: Retrain If You Have To!

From my interaction with many single mothers, lack of proper education is probably one of the top hindrances to their pursuit of financial freedom. Everyday we see the growing phenomenon of younger single mothers in our generation. Even today, there are single mothers who got pregnant while they were in high school, and they quit school either out of embarrassment or family's discouragement or for other social reasons. Many of these women remain at the same educational level, even decades after they left school, and have practically given up! I've heard quite some excuses. Top among them is; "Oh, I'm too old now, I can't go back to high school; forget it Rose; no way!"

Attack Your Excuses: Face Short-Term Hurdles for Long-Term Benefits!

My question is this: what are you embarrassed about? That younger students will laugh at you if you went back to school? By all means, let them laugh and make fun! It's ***your*** future you want to work on, not theirs! By the way, even if they laugh, it's only ***temporary***; consider it an *interrupt* and put it on your ***Interrupt Page***! Then develop strategies to ***not*** let their mockery get to you!

Think about this: if you spent the next year or two working on your high school diploma, what would prevent you from going on to College to get a diploma or a degree? Or if you go back to College and finish your degree program, what could stop you from getting a Masters degree or a Ph.D.? If you're worried about high-school students, did you know that by the time you get to College, the age difference doesn't even show that much any more? So why give up on a lifetime of fulfilled dreams for only a short time of embarrassment?

The bottom line is this: if you've always wanted to be a lawyer, by all means, go to law school! Have you always wanted to be a doctor? Brush up on your Biology, Physics, and Chemistry, and please get cracking! Don't let anything or any excuse stop you!

Don't Let Age Be a Barrier, Because It's Not!

There's no age limit to getting a good education. Why feel embarrassed about returning to school later in life? I rather look at older people who are going to school as models of encouragement and challenge to the younger ones; they should feel very proud of themselves, and not embarrassed at all! In fact, my neighbor went back to school two years ago, to get a University degree – get this: she's 83 years old! Am I impressed? Way beyond your imagination! For an eighty-three-year-old woman to go back to school just to fulfill her dreams, it takes nothing but courage, wisdom, smartness, and everything good! She should win many medals just for that one item alone.

No matter how old you are, there is education available to you ***if and only if*** you reach out and take it. You must take the steps yourself; no one else can do it for you. Please take advantage of the many government provisions for single mothers in the educational sector. In some countries, you can actually get your College degree for free simply because you're a single mother! Take advantage of these programs, and fulfill your dreams!

Invest in Your Future! Stop the 'Spend Attacks'!

"Savings" should be a top item in every single mother's ***Working Page***. Most of us are broke most of the time! Tell me about that! ☺. I hear a lot of, "I don't make enough money to put food on the table; where in the world will the savings come from?" It seems a reasonable argument, but my financial attitude changed dramatically when I attended a financial seminar in Toronto, a few years ago. In that seminar the speaker focused on the things we think don't cost money, but on which we spend money on a very regular basis, thereby hindering our ability to save or invest for the future.

Many of us go on frequent spending frenzies, what I call a 'spend attack', and we buy many things we don't *really need*, and maybe never even use! We also encourage or allow our children to push us into buying things for them simply because 'everyone in school has it'. We however need to get our spending habits in order, and concentrate on building a more solid financial future both for ourselves and for the children.

One thing that comes to mind very quickly for us girls is fashion. The question you need to answer a few times is: how much do I spend on clothes, shoes, makeovers, makeup, and so on? Could I cut back on those expenses and put aside say $20, $50, or more a month? I'm being quite conservative with these figures, and I bet you many single mothers can put much more aside every month if they cut back on makeup alone, or shoes for that matter.

Another thing that eats deep into the pockets without your knowing is snacks. They look cheap, even 'innocent', but they cost quite a lot when you look at the bigger picture of monthly expenses on the chocolate bars, pop, gum, candies, and so on. If you cut back on snacks, you could possibly put another $50 away per month!

The idea here is for you to make a list of the things you spend your money on every month, and look for places to cut back without affecting the well-being of yourself and the kids. Add this to your ***Working Page***, and make a resolve to cut back on these so you can save more money. One way I look at snacks is that they are not even good for me, at least most of them. Now I focus on eating well, and it's much easier to cut back on the snacks and extra fat!

Try College Funds and Mutual Funds

As a single mother, I challenge you to begin to consider the future of your children and their education. Here in Canada, if you invest in an RESP (Registered Education Savings Plan), the government adds a certain percentage to your yearly savings for each child (as at 2003, the Canadian government adds 20% up to a maximum of $400.00 each year). We must recognize that the cost of education is always on the rise; "it ain't gonna get cheaper." If you invest in your children's education every month, even if it's $20 a month, you go a long way in making it easier for them to get proper education when it's College time. Again I'm being conservative with the figures. I believe many of us can do much better than $20, so begin to save up for the future.

Moreover, if you put some money aside for yourself each month in form of an RSP (talk to your financial planner, but try mutual funds for long-term investments), you increase your chances of living a much more comfortable life when it's retirement time, by God's Grace. The failure to save now is an indirect way of guaranteeing that you'll live in poverty the rest of your life, simply because you spend everything you have today.

The other thing to watch against is your ex's prophecy, 'you cannot make it without me!' Would you just sit back and let that prophecy fulfill itself in your life? I say, "NO!" You can make it! But you've got to invest. If you have never invested before, I suggest you put that on your ***Working Page*** and start today. Watch your finances grow slowly but surely, and you can pay me my commission later. Trust me, it's fun to invest, and it's rewarding for your children. Please go and talk to your banker today, or get a Financial Planner, and get started!

Tithing Unlocks the Doors of Financial Success!

In Malachi 3:8-12, the Lord says to His people:

> ***Will a man rob God? Yet you have robbed me. But you say, wherein have we robbed you? In tithes and offerings. You are cursed with a curse, for you have robbed me, even this whole nation. Bring all the tithes into the storehouse, that there may be meat in my house, and prove me now herewith, says the Lord of hosts, if I will not open for you the windows of heaven, and pour you out a blessing that there shall not be room enough to receive it. And I will rebuke the devourer for your sakes, and he shall not destroy the fruits of your***

> ***ground, neither shall your vine cast her fruit before the time in the fields, says the Lord of hosts: and all nations shall call you blessed, for you shall be a delightsome land, says the Lord of hosts.***

If you work and earn income, it's important to thank God who gave it to you, by paying your tithe (only 10%) to your church. As the Lord Himself explains in Malachi 3, He will rebuke the devourer for your sake if you pay your tithes. He will also remove a spiritual curse from you, your land or country.

There are many ways we allow the devil to torment us even though we go to church every week. For example, your kids could suddenly get sick for no clear reason; then you would be forced to pay for doctor's visits and medicine for them. Your car could suddenly break down and you'll have to pay your mechanic. Things could break down in the house, and so on. When things like these happen, check your tithing life.

If you're not paying your tithes to the Lord's house in appreciation for what He has done for you, the devourer would come in and punch large holes in your spiritual pockets, and they'll begin to leak into unexpected expenses!

For the Lord's protection for us as we come in and go out, the least we can do is pay our tithes. After all, He opened the doors of opportunities to us and gave us our jobs, so really, what's the quarrel with tithing? We must demonstrate gratitude to God by tithing as He commands us. In the long run, it's actually for your own sake, your own protection. If you are faithful to God, He would put a hedge of protection around you, and keep you from the evil one. May the Lord help us as we obey His word.

Also, the Lord says in Luke 6:38:

> ***Give and it shall be given to you, good measure, pressed down, and shaken together, and running over, shall men give into your bosom. For with the same measure that you mete, withal it shall be measured to you again.***

When you begin to be faithful to God in the area of tithes and offerings in His house, your finances will begin to improve. God will cause promotions and opportunities to come your way more than ever before. God will also cause your investments to have high returns. I've found this to be true in my life. Try Him and see. Tithing actually works! It doesn't reduce you. It enlarges your coasts because God will release the forces of heaven to start looking out and working for you. Tithing is the key that unlocks the doors to financial success!

Chapter 8. Maintain A Healthy Lifestyle.

As a single mother, part of feeling good about yourself stems from how physically active you are in terms of exercise. It's important to exercise on a regular basis. There is a wrong notion that exercise is for the chubby ladies like I was then, but your doctor would tell you correctly that exercise is important for everyone! Whether you're overweight or not, you need to exercise to enable your heart and other organs work optimally, and for smooth blood flow through your body vessels.

Walking, for example, is a great way to exercise. Read up or ask your doctor and you'll discover that even 30 minutes walk a day can help you maintain a very healthy heart. Summer is a great time to walk everyday, and sometimes I envy my friends in Africa, because they can walk in the heat and have no problems with being overweight. For people in temperate countries, it's a little more difficult in the winter, but you can always exercise indoors when you have five feet of snow outside! For example, some people take their walks in malls or shopping centers.

Try Gym Membership

Some people can exercise on their own in their own homes. If you can, lucky you! I tried to exercise in my home many times, and it was usually hilariously ineffective! As soon as I put my music on for step aerobics, my children would all rush in and I'll have feet, hands and legs flying all over the place! Or if I hopped on a bike, I would have one kid on one side, another behind the pedal, kids all over! It was fun, but not very efficient for me, so I decided to take the group exercise or gym approach.

My first gym membership was at a big facility in which many of my co-workers worked out. I excitedly took an annual membership that cost me $480, in 1998. Then I visited the gym steadily for about a month or so, and finally my zeal sizzled off completely. I tried to get my money back but of course it was no use. I had a one-year contract and my fees were non-refundable! I let it go, smarted for some months, and then decided to try another strategy.

After analyzing my first gym-membership experience, I realized that jumping into an annual contract might not be very helpful for a new exercise convert. What I did after that was to go to a less expensive facility that had what I wanted: step classes (aerobics). First I signed up for one month. I got myself slowly into a pattern (once a week, then twice a week), and then signed up for 3 months. When I had worked myself into a regular pattern, where I went to the gym more frequently and regularly, then I paid for an annual membership.

Another problem with my first gym membership was that I signed up with a really big but expensive popular 'brand-name' gym. It's actually not necessary to do that. It's important to identify the types of exercise you need, and you shouldn't allow yourself to pay for one thousand other equipment you may never use. For me, if a gym has cardio-aerobics classes, that's all I need. Now I do limited weight training, but when I started, I got really inexpensive deals because I stayed with small gyms that had my step aerobics classes.

Maintain a Healthy Diet

Exercising is really important; but we need to compliment that with a good, ***healthy*** diet. Everyone, especially single mothers with young children, need lots of energy for the many physical and mental activities that we engage in.

I am aware that many 'diets' abound, but I suggest that you make sure you eat well. The emphasis should not be on losing weight, but on being *healthy.* Don't sacrifice good health in exchange for a slim look.

There is a lot of information about health in bookstores and grocery stores around you. Don't go for any so-called diet plan that promises to give you fast weight loss. If you lose weight fast, chances are that you'll gain it all back; easy come easy go.

Talk to your doctor. Personally, what has worked for me has been to eat lots of fruits and vegetables, and to replace pop with water. In the last 12 months, I have successfully kept off 25lbs, but that's a different story.

Since individual bodies differ, it's important to go with a reasonable diet that works for you, as long as it's healthy. Combine that with exercise, and you'll have the physical strength to cope with the multi-faced challenge of raising children on your own.

Improve Your Physical Appearance

As we discuss self-improvement, let us not forget our physical *appearance.* Not weight or height, but the way we appear to others around us, and the way we dress, our hair, the shoes we wear, everything on the outside apart from our bodily structure. We need to improve on our physical appearance, so we can feel better about ourselves, irrespective of how others feel.

For example, during my 'mirror-mirror-on-the-wall" sessions, I 'graduated' from telling myself in the mirror, "God has given me good hair", to "Okay, I really have good hair, but I think I need to perm it or go to the salon and do something about it." I began to identify places on my body that needed improvement. First thing of course was my weight, then I moved on to my hair!

Naturally, the primary focus is different for each person, so you need to prioritize your self-improvement program, put items on your Working Page, and take them one at a time. Mama Rose had practically handed me over to Joy, my hairdresser in Toronto, and given her instructions to ***work on*** my hair. So I booked an appointment with Joy. The first time I went, I said, "Do whatever you think suits me, Joy. I honestly don't have any ideas!" She was very excited; she loved challenges and really, my hair was quite a challenge! Joy relaxed and curled my hair, trimmed and styled it. The next Sunday morning, many people did not recognize me! I got lots and lots of compliments! That was something and it made me feel soooo gooooood!

Next, I decided that I needed a facial. So I got one. Then I decided to begin to use makeup on a regular and more informed basis. The Lord brought me in the way of beloved sisters, who taught me to take good care of my face. I learned very slowly, but I learned. I began to nurture my face from the dry, cracked and pimple-ridden face to a more moisturized, smoother one. Bottom-line, I began to find ways to improve myself. When you start on this project, your self-esteem will shoot to the sky! I say, "Go for it, girl!"

Change Your Wardrobe!

Someone might say, "Oh, you're beautiful, it doesn't matter what you wear". There are some people who have such God-endowed beauty that the above statement works for them. For the rest of us, including myself, we need to work a little harder than that.

I decided that my wardrobe had to change. I wanted to look good but I owned mostly baggy clothes. I wonder if that identifies with you. When you think you are ugly, you would wear baggy clothes to cover up the perceived ugliness. But once I got past that and felt better about my weight, I wanted to wear *clothes that fit!* I wanted to show off the new me.

I slowly began to change my wardrobe. Trust me, this part is an expensive one, but the trick is to start very slowly, one paycheck at a time. Another trick is to replace everything you have with inexpensive clothes, and slowly begin to buy a more expensive, longer-lasting wardrobe as your finances let you. Whichever approach you choose, the goal is to look good at a reasonable cost, not extravagantly! Please don't sell your electronics to buy clothes. I believe that it's not your dressing that's most important; it's how you carry yourself and how you feel about yourself. Start with carrying yourself like a queen. Then you can slowly stock up on the wardrobe.

Carrying Yourself Like A Queen

My friend Lara used to say to me, "It's not what you wear, but how you wear it. Also it's not how you wear your clothes, but how you carry yourself." I agree with her one hundred percent.

Two women can wear identical outfits, but one can look sloppy and the other looks elegant. The difference? Gait and posture.

Did you know that people sometimes treat you based on the way you carry yourself? Your gait suggests your level of confidence. If you carry yourself with a shoulder hunch or lowered head, (maybe erroneously, but still) people could misinterpret that to mean low self-esteem. If you study the psychology of bullies, they usually target others whom they perceive are weak and lack confidence, usually by the way they carry themselves.

Learn to carry and comport yourself like a queen. The word of God tells us in I Peter 2:9:

> ***But you are a chosen generation, a royal priesthood, a holy nation, a peculiar people; that you should show forth the praises of Him who has called you out of darkness into His marvelous light.***

You are a daughter of the King of kings! Carry yourself with dignity! Hold your head up high! And change the way people relate with you.

Take a break! Go pamper yourself!

Do you sometimes feel that you're burnt out, and really, really need a break? I do! Have you ever caught yourself sleeping behind the steering because you're so tired, yet you must still go do your groceries or run that extra errand? I have! Sometimes I look at the pace at which I'm going and I get so exhausted that I hate my life. When I feel this way, I begin to snap at my children and begin to feel that they are responsible for my fatigue. I get really irritable and I just want to throw everyone away! But the Lord brought beloved sisters my way who taught me that I must set some time aside for myself.

It's important to put aside some 'me' time ***everyday***, when you can be all alone, not necessarily sleeping when the kids are playing or doing their homework, but just be by yourself to meditate, shower, just stare at the ceiling, whatever you want! If you have kids of school age and you have some time during the day, your personal time could be when the kids are at school. For the rest of us who have full-time jobs or full-time school, and who come home same time as the kids, you have no choice but create personal time when the kids are home from school. This is a bit more challenging, but the trick is to start the routine and the children will eventually know that "Mum can't come to the phone right now; she's resting".

Yes, your personal time means you can't take telephone calls! Sometimes people who just can't stop talking could call, and if you take those calls during your personal time, you won't get any rest at all. Tell your friends that it's not a good time to call; they'll get used to it. I'm speaking of just one hour each day, and if that's the only time someone chooses to call, that's too bad.

Apart from daily personal time, you also need to take at least one weekend off every now and then. If you can give yourself one weekend off each month, that's super! For me, one weekend every other month works wonders, but I wish I could get one per month; it's still a target my kids and I need to work out. My idea for the weekend off is to send the kids away from home, and for you to go away by yourself if you can afford it. If you can't afford to go away by yourself, sending the kids away would be sufficient. This plan works for me with a double-edged sword: first, the kids go out of their familiar environment and when they come back, it's like they've been on a vacation. They return with new energy and enthusiasm. For me, it gives me time to pamper myself and do whatever I want while the kids are gone.

Please remember that your personal time off is NOT time to clean the house or do laundry or other housework, but just time to rejuvenate yourself, away from the kids, cooking and all the familiar "friendly" noise. You can pray, meditate, eat, sleep, listen to music, and prepare yourself for the month ahead.

The Lord whom I serve is such a good God; He takes care of every facet of our lives, no matter how insignificant it seems. The Lord blessed me with such good friends and neighbors and brothers and sisters in the Church, that fatigue is not a problem for me any longer. I have a beloved sister, Deborah, who came to me one day and asked to take all my kids for a weekend. She said she loves them so much, she wanted to have 5 kids of her own! I looked at her and knew she had no idea what in the world she was saying. On that Friday night, I gladly sent the kids over to Deborah's for the weekend. Of course by Saturday morning, Deborah called me to come get all my kids (they were so much trouble!), but I had turned off my phone and she left a message. By the time they came back on Sunday, Deborah was more exhausted than she had ever been, and she had reduced the number of kids she wants to have from 5 all the way down to 1! And of course she added the usual compliment, "I don't know how you do it!" I always take that as a medal.

My kids went to Deborah's so many times for weekends, it became their second home. Also they had sleepovers with lots of other 'aunties' and 'uncles' from the church and our local community.

My reason for expanding on this subject is to drive home the point that you need to set aside some 'me' time when you can be alone all by yourself, without any interruption or demands from the children. If you don't give yourself personal time, you could end up in a fatigue cycle that will be detrimental both to yourself and to the children.

Find some friends with whom you can leave the children for a day or two. Then go away and pamper yourself! Go to the spa, get a massage, get a manicure and pedicure, anything! Just give yourself some personal time and rejuvenate yourself. You'll find that if you get even one weekend off each quarter, fatigue would be quite far away from you.

Chapter 9. Nurture A Mother – Child Partnership

Train up a child in the way he should go: and when he is old he will not depart from it (Proverbs 22:6)

How about the children? The children are at the center of all our preceding discussion, and as we have seen in previous chapters, we must strive to lay down good examples for them to follow and also to develop ourselves so we can take better care of them "single-handedly", so to say.

What does it mean then to take care of your children? Is it sufficient to set food on the table and buy them clothes and shoes? My answer to that is a big "NO".

Take a look around your neighborhood. Look at some of the children you call 'naughty' in your mind. Why do you think they behave naughtily? Would you want your children to behave like the naughty ones?

Listen to the news. It's mostly bad news. When you see juvenile delinquents on television, what do you think? If in your heart you're afraid your kids could end up like them, then this chapter is for you.

I'll like you to try the ***Personal Pickup / Progress Challenge*** again, this time for your children. Think back to when you were a child. What were your dreams for your own children? What were some of the behaviors you swore you would never let your children see, experience, or execute? Are you living up to those aspirations? Do you perceive that your children could be living the same way you swore they would never live and for some reason, you've allowed yourself to not clean up?

These are heart-burning questions, but take the challenge and address them. As far as children are concerned, it's never too late to point them in the right direction. Of course it's much easier when they are younger, but even if they're delinquent already, you can still win them over, by the power of the Lord Jesus Christ.

In this chapter I'll address several issues relating to the way I pursued my children's welfare. Many times people tell me, "Rose, your children are so well-behaved, how do you do it?" My usual incredulous response is, "Them? Well-behaved? Hmmm..." But when I really stop to think about it, I know my children have come a very long way. People who knew us from Toronto would say that they have "changed a lot!" That is very true. However, like any other long journey, it's never achieved in one day, but with patience, tender love, and moulding, with God's help.

First, Take Them for Counseling

One mistake I find some of my fellow single mothers make is the neglect of their children's psychological welfare. Usually, it's because they think the kids don't need counseling. I have heard many times, "They're kids;

they are resilient; they will recover."

Unfortunately, children are often the most hard-hit in a broken home, especially if they are older and perceptive when their parents' marriage breaks down. If a child has seen parents fight or quarrel constantly, that child is a very good candidate for post-separation counseling.

When my marriage broke down, I took my children down to the North York General Hospital's Children's Counseling Clinic for weeks of counseling. At that time, Jerry was only 5 years old; and he had 4 younger siblings aged 4, 3, 1, and 2 months! The boy was traumatized, and it was quite a good thing that I took them all for counseling. We left out Gabby (the youngest) since she wasn't old enough to know whatever was happening. Peace and Emmanuel talked quite a bit to the counselors about what they had seen and heard, and of course talking is therapeutic all by itself. However, the counselors found that Jerry internalized many things – he wouldn't talk initially. After several weeks of counseling, he slowly opened up and began to talk about his understanding of what had taken place between Mum and Dad. They found that he was angry, scared, and felt rejected all at the same time. It took us quite a long time to get him to deal with those emotions effectively. Quite a challenge for a five-year-old, but Jerry's a tough kid and he's pulling through still.

There are some moments even now that he's much older, when those feelings still come up, and I must put everything aside and listen to him, and reassure him that I love him, that his Dad loves him too, and no matter what happens, I will never leave him, nor his brother and sisters. Had I not taken them through expert counseling, I wouldn't have learnt how to handle some of the emotions my children display today.

Counseling for kids should not be considered a one-time event. As the children in a broken home grow up, they have lots of questions that the single mother may not be able to answer effectively. Several things go through their minds that they may not even discuss at all. If left unchecked, these thoughts could develop and hinder their normal psychological development. So as they grow, it's important to take them out for counseling, I'll suggest, once a year (or semi-annually if you think it's necessary).

God Has a Special Interest in Your Children

In the beginning of this book, I shared with you the Lord's promise in Isaiah 40:11:

> ***[God] shall feed His flock like a shepherd; He shall gather the lambs with His arm, and carry them in His bosom, and shall gently lead those that are with young.***

God is especially interested in the welfare of young children, and Jesus confirms the Father's soft spot in Matthew 19:14, Luke 18:16-17, and Matthew 18:2-6, 10:

> ***But Jesus said, Suffer little children, and forbid them not, to come unto me: for of such is the kingdom of heaven...*** *(Matthew 19:14, Luke 18:16)*

> ***Verily I say unto you, whosoever shall not receive the kingdom of God as a little child shall in no wise enter***

> ***therein.*** *(Luke 18:17)*
>
> ***Take heed that you despise not one of these little one; for I say unto you, that in heaven their angels do always behold the face of my Father which is in heaven.*** *(Matthew 18:10).*
>
> ***And Jesus called a little child unto Him and set him in the midst of them, and said, Verily I say to you, except you be converted and become as little children, you shall not enter into the kingdom of heaven. Whosoever therefore shall humble himself as this little child, the same is the greatest in the kingdom of God, and whoso shall receive one such little child in my name receives me.*** *(Matthew 18:2-5).*

Paul, by the Holy Spirit, confirms this in Ephesians 6: 1-4:

> ***Children, obey your parents in the Lord; for this is right. Honor your father and mother, which is the first commandment with promise; that it may be well with you, and that you may live long on the earth. And you fathers*** *(I'll add mothers),* ***provoke not your children to wrath: but bring them up in the nurture and admonition of the Lord.***

Many of us remember to cite Ephesians 6:1-3 to our children, "honor your father and mother…", but we totally forget that the Lord also commands us to not provoke them to wrath, but to bring them up in the nurture, direction and admonition of the Lord.

For me, one of the most frightening scriptures about the special love of God for little children is the one following Matthew 18:2-5:

> ***But whoso shall offend one of these little ones which believe in me, it were better for him that a millstone***

were hanged around his neck, and that he were in the depth of the sea! *(Matthew 18:6)*

When many of us read this scripture, we quickly think of pedophiles or bullies and other child molesters. We forget to think of ourselves as parents and the many ways we offend our children!

So, stop and think again about Matthew 18:6. What does it mean to 'offend' your child? I actually took some time to study this scriptural direction to not offend my children, and what I discovered during my times of meditation was simply phenomenal! It blew my mind! Please come on this journey with me, and I pray the Lord will open your eyes, if you were in the same situation I was with my children before the Lord gave me this discovery.

What does it mean to 'offend' your child?

According to the Merriam-Webster Dictionary, to offend means many things, including the following:

to transgress the moral or divine law; to do wrong, or violate a law or rule

to cause difficulty, discomfort, pain, or injury

to cause dislike, anger, or vexation <like using reckless words>

to cause to sin or fall

to cause to feel vexation, hurt feelings or deep resentment usually by violation of what is proper or fitting <like using bad language>

a synonym of 'offend' is ***affront***, which implies treating with deliberate rudeness or contemptuous indifference to courtesy

another synonym is ***insult*** which suggests deliberately causing humiliation, hurt pride, or shame

Quite a lot of meaning for a seemingly simple word, but we need to examine the word ***offend*** with respect to our relationships with our children. Let us analyze the above meanings in bits and pieces. Let's pay attention to the more subtle meanings, rather than the most obvious like #2. The reason I'm doing this is because many times, we ignore some 'secondary' meanings of words, concentrate on popular meanings, and lose out on the efficacy of watching out for things that we think are of less importance but which carry such weight with little children, it is quite interesting.

Most parents look at 'offending a child' as parts of meaning #2 in the above list, that is, "to cause pain or injury". Unfortunately, it's much, much deeper than that. To deliberately injure or hurt a child is definitely wrong, and when you deliberately injure your child, you step into the same position as a pedophile, really. Think about that.

Moreover, the Lord revealed to me that one of the biggest reasons we parents, especially single mothers, fail in raising our children, is because we miss the root of relationships: partnership.

Mother-Child Partnership is Key to Successful Parenting

One of the most amazing things the Lord showed me as I prayed about my relationship with my children was that I must cultivate a partnership with them!

My first argument was, 'Partnership? But I'm supposed to be in charge; I should be the leader, put them in their right positions…" But the Lord impressed it upon my heart that it must be a partnership, for many reasons.

The Bible says in Amos 3:3, "***can two walk together except they agree?***" We mostly look at this scripture from the perspective of husband-wife, corporate, business, or other adult relationships. But do you know that the same applies to your children? They may be young, but they are human too. They are very smart, much smarter than you think sometimes. They also have amazingly sharp spiritual perception, and what's more, God is especially interested in them.

Why do you think marriages break down? Simple: because the partners do not 'agree' on fundamental or essential issues. When a husband and wife do not think on the same plane, or treat each other with respect, or walk in deliberate ***partnership***, they begin to slowly head for the rocks.

Partnership in any relationship, be it business or

personal, means that both parties purposefully work together for the mutual benefit of the entity that the relationship represents. They work towards a common goal. They look out for each other. They suggest ways of improvement. They help the partners to know ways to relate to them better. They make up their minds and are determined to keep the partnership and make it succeed. Even when trouble comes as they always do, the partners come together and discuss a jointly-decided way to resolve or mitigate the problem. Each partner has a mental resolve to make the partnership work. This is the case, regardless of whether it's a home or a business.

If, on the other hand, there is no partnership in the real sense, one person selfishly seeks his or her own benefits at the detriment of the other. Things are not discussed and agreed upon. Decisions get taken without the other's approval or permission. One person sabotages the other. When trouble comes, resolving it becomes a mountainous task, and things slowly get out of hand.

Based on my experience with my own children, I want to put it to you that creating mother-child partnership is the key to your success as a single mother. If you as a single mother do not relate to your children with respect, you won't agree on many things and won't create a partnership. The children will begin to feel that they are really not part of what is going on, and slowly they begin to drift away from you and home.

If, on the other hand, you create a partnership with them, they would warm up to you, and you would be quite amazed at the ideas they come up with sometimes. When

I started having little 'family meetings' with my children, they were first amused, then they felt quite important and they began to give me ideas on how to deal with them better, how to organize the house, chore-allocation strategies, intelligent ideas! When they understood that I wanted them to work ***with*** me, their behavior towards me changed to a more mature, loving one. It was quite a transformation! God is truly the God of wisdom!

You think children don't divorce their parents? Think again!

If you were in a physically abusive marriage like I was, think about when your spouse used you as a punching bag. Did that make you feel like you were in partnership with him? Of course not! When a woman is hurt and insulted by a spouse, she leaves the relationship *mentally*. Even if there is no legal separation or divorce, the marriage is actually over – mentally. However, as grown ups, we can take one step further and go through the legal system and acquire a divorce. That's because we have the maturity and financial ability to go through the trouble of legalizing the way we feel.

On the other hand, children don't have the know-how or ability to pursue a divorce from their parents. Unfortunately though, many children actually divorce from their parents *mentally*.

The first time I thought about this, I was shocked! But it is so true. When you as a mother hurl hateful words and insults at your child, you violate the child's feelings and self-respect and you cause vexation, humiliation, and hateful feelings in the child. Following our dictionary definition, that is “offense”. In your child’s mind, if he or she could get far away from you, they would! However, because they can’t fend for themselves, they stay *unwillingly.*

I’ve heard lots of children say, ‘as soon as I’m 16, I’m out of here!’ Do you think it’s because of the attainment of the age of responsibility? Many times not. If you look deeply, it’s because they’ve divorced their parents mentally, and will physically remove themselves as soon as they can. These children may never come back in the real sense of relationships.

One big reason for children’s mental divorce of a parent is because they perceive the parent as an enemy! Really? When an abused woman gets punched and battered by her spouse, does she consider him as a friend or as an enemy? Definitely as an enemy that hates her and wants to really hurt her. In the same way, if children perceive through hurtful words or actions, that their mother doesn’t like them, they consider that mother an enemy, and would do anything to get away from her. While they live with that mother, abused children could even go a step further to sabotage their mother’s efforts as a parent!

So the key is to develop strategies to be your children’s friend. Work with them in partnership and your work as Mum would be much easier to handle.

Developing Your Partnership

The way this works for me may not be the way you decide, but again, my emphasis is on developing some kind of partnership with your children. For example, I made Jerry my *Executive Vice President*! He felt so important that he initially started to beat up on the younger ones! Slowly though, he learnt that 'beating up siblings' is not part of the job description of an Executive Vice-President. But the fact that I put him in charge of some things made him feel really important and helped his self-esteem a great deal.

Then I appointed everyone else to different roles – Secretary, Financial Advisor, Home Management Advisor, Health Manager, and so on. We plan most things together, from meals to vacations. I make a big deal about everything and we have at least one 'meeting' a week. Basically, the meetings help us to discuss as a team, and even though I may have a very clear idea what I want to do and only use the meetings to get their consensus, yet it gives them a very good sense of participating in the events and running of the home – a partnership indeed.

During these meetings, I actually find that my kids come up with excellent ideas and suggestions as to how to manage the home, how to spend, and so on. With Peace as my Financial Advisor for example, I find that the demands for vogue things from their school or friends dropped drastically. I find that she encourages her siblings to consider how much things cost, and to focus on food and clothing rather than unnecessarily expensive toys.

When it comes to discipline, we discuss it as a team, and each sibling chips in his or her ideas as to how *we* should discipline a culprit. It's a joint decision and of course sometimes I have the veto power as the *CEO and President*, but it works better when they are involved in deciding their own punishments. The other thing this does is that each child is kinder to their siblings at discipline time because they know it could be their turn tomorrow, so they actually come up with reasonable disciplinary ideas!

Also when it comes to cleanup time, I assign *Inspectors* and *Policemen* to each room. One sibling cleans, another inspects to ensure that the work was done properly, and the person who cleans is the responsible Policeman or Policewoman for his or her own sanitation territory! In my home, this works like magic. Try it, and you will find that if you assign them tasks as partners in the business of building and maintaining your home, your work as Mum would encounter much fewer hassles.

Create Partnership with the Children's Schools

Partnership with your child also involves partnership with the people that help to mould their personalities. The children's schools belong to this category. Working with teachers in a *positive* manner to foster an environment for balanced education for your children, is a salient aspect of mother-child partnership. There are certain areas of your child's life that you should take care of yourself. However, their school teachers are the best qualified to handle education and classroom instruction.

Partnership with your children's school involves working with the teachers to determine what areas your child needs help the most. My strategy is to support my children's teachers by helping at home with homework and projects. In turn their teachers support me by letting me know any unusual or lazy behavior that my children exhibit in the classroom. This way I get good feedback and I can deal with issues before they take deep root. I thank God for my teachers at Cedarbrae School, Calgary. They are excellent! They send me feedback on any behavioral deviations in my children as soon as they happen, and as experienced parents themselves, they give me hints on how to handle unfamiliar territory. There are many things I couldn't possibly do without *my teachers.*

I have seen some mothers who get all upset about a teacher's discipline to their child, and I wonder about that because in most cases the teachers mean very well. These mothers forget that complaining about a teacher's discipline is *not* good for the child because it tells that child that s/he can do whatever s/he wants in class and expect to get away with it! If you do this, you must not be surprised when that same child will refuse *your* own discipline because "what's good for the teacher is good for Mum as well!"

It's very important to work with your children's teachers in partnership, to present a *common* front of discipline to the children, so they know that if they get into trouble at school, they're "really gonna get it" when they get home. Parent-teacher partnership is particularly helpful to single mothers because at home, we don't have a resident 'dad'; the teachers at school help us to some extent with a firm disciplinary program.

Partnership with your children's school also involves volunteering for in-class activities or excursions. I cannot over-emphasize the need for parents, particularly single mothers, to make time to volunteer in the children's school(s). Being 'around' helps the children psychology, and sends them a good message: "Mum cares about my education". For example, I notice that when I go to my children's classes, they perk up, they pay more attention to their work, and they are quicker to participate in class activities with more energy. This tells me that my presence does have a positive psychological effect on them, which in turn affects their attitudes to their school work. Sometimes that's all you really need to do to get them to love school!

I recognize that sometimes work schedules do not permit mothers to visit their children's schools, but as much as possible, it's important to make out some time, even if it's just for thirty minutes a week. You'll see the difference it makes in your child's interest in school.

Homework Trouble?

Although I've mentioned homework as part of partnership with the children's schools, I want to spend some more time to discuss the need to *proactively* assist your children in tackling their homework.

I have talked to some mothers who neglect to help their children with homework. When I ask why, I actually get some *seemingly reasonable* answers like "I don't speak French, so I can't help him there", or it could be Math, or something else.

Unfortunately, if you don't pay attention to your child's homework, they could get the psychological impression that you don't care about their education, and so you don't have any right to tell them to improve in school if they do badly. I thank God that I speak some French and I love Math, and I can supervise my kids in practically all their homework, but I had an interesting experience in Toronto that helped me adopt the strategy I recommend to some of the mothers I discuss with.

In the 1999/2000 academic session, I enrolled my children in the Weekend Mandarin Language School, organized by the International Language Program of the Greater Toronto Board of Education. The first day we got there, the Registration Officer, a lovely Chinese lady, asked us what we wanted. I answered her, "I want what you're offering: I want to enroll my kids in your school". She actually burst out into a long laugh. I joined her, and we both laughed and laughed. I knew exactly where she was coming from – no one expected a Nigerian family to enroll in the Mandarin language school! But when we finished laughing, I said to her, "Seriously, could we please proceed with our registration?" She looked at my face and knew I was serious. We registered and embarked on a very interesting year! My kids found it fun, and by the end of the year, each of my children was in the top 10 of their classes! Unbelievable! Even one teacher told me she was completely intrigued.

How did we do it? It was my idea to enroll them in Mandarin school, and so I had to take the extra challenge to help them with the homework they brought home each Saturday. I never knew any Mandarin, couldn't decipher the hieroglyphics, but I started to discuss with the teachers and they taught me basic Mandarin conversation, which I can still use today! Then I picked up a computer-based learning software on Chinese that was channeled more towards the structured Mandarin than the less-structured Cantonese and I learned a little bit. Then I worked with my children every weekend on their homework, and the things I didn't know, they taught me! In the process, they got their homework done. It was fun to watch them perform Mandarin dances and songs at the end of the school year!

What I am trying to put across to us mothers is this: you can help your children with their homework, no matter the subject. The trick is to create a regular homework time, and sit at the table with them. For us, because of all our evening activities, we do homework from 4-5pm weekdays, before our evening rat race begins. We also use the early part of Saturdays if we have some leftover from the weekdays. If you can't help them with Math, ask them to show you what they are doing. Ask your neighbor to show you, or get a self-learning kit from the library. If you work on it, you'll get it; and maybe your children could end up teaching you, but they'll get their homework done and they'll know you're really interested in their education. Take up the challenge. If I could do it with Mandarin, I'm sure you can do it with Math!

Develop Partnership with Your Neighbors

Another group of people you may want to partner with (if appropriate) is your next-door neighbors, or co-residents on the same street, or anyone you feel comfortable with who lives *close* to you in the same neighborhood. I have chosen my words carefully here because there are some neighbors who are not friendly, and you want to stay away from those. There are some people who make it their job to spy on your comings-in and goings-out, for gossip purposes only: stay away from those as well!

One reason it's important to have a *reliable* and *friendly* neighbor to partner with is for emergencies. For example, if I am in the middle of cooking a meal and I run out of salt (this is a common example), I can go to my next-door neighbor and get some!

I thank God for my neighbors: Lina Beaulieu has three children, Les and Maryanne Tomso have a son, Karol has a grandson, Dave Gano and Kerry Barnes have two sons, Wendy and Wes have four children (one of whom is like my own daughter), Ivorine Bell has two children, and I have five. Collectively, our children don't ever lack play-partners! It's always a busy street!

The good thing about my neighbors is that we've developed such partnership that we look out for each other's children; we talk to them as to our own, and if anyone needs to run to the store in a hurry, we take care of their children. If anyone travels, we take care of their pets. It's almost like raising a child in my African village where everyone looks out for everyone else. My neighbors and I help each other out with areas in which we have great skills; I help with computers and I stopped counting how many times my neighbors have helped me mow the lawns, fix the bicycles, anything! Neighbors like that are hard to come by, and if I didn't have great neighbors, I would have moved long ago.

Neighborly Partnerships Help Prevent Unnecessary Disasters

I must stress the need to have neighborly partnerships because they go a long way to helping a single mother to coordinate *emergency* childcare. I thank God that my Mom is here to help a great deal, but most single mothers don't have that extra advantage.

Children are very adventurous, and when unsupervised, they come up with the most dangerous flashes of ideas! All of a sudden, they remember that they've always wanted to cook up a storm, or fill up the Jacuzzi for a nice warm soak, or call 911, … anything! The minute you turn your back, something is bound to go wrong. In extreme cases, you could have a disaster that's just waiting to happen … unless you've arranged with your good neighbors to have these very creative children under constant supervision. It's therefore very important to have properly organized neighborly partnerships where everyone pools resources together to watch out for one another's children and homes. Knowing that you can't do it all on your own, this network of neighbors is a very powerful resource for single mothers.

One incident particularly comes to mind in support of the need for neighborly partnerships. One Sunday morning we left for church about 8am, and I was baking some chicken for dinner, with the plan to turn off the oven when we returned from church by 1pm. I had however forgotten that we had a lunch date about a half-hour-drive away from home. In the middle of lunch, I remembered my chicken was still in the oven! Normally, that would have been the end of our lunch date; I would have panicked and rushed all the way back home. However, my neighbor Kerry has a key to my house, and all I did was call her and she very graciously went in and turned off my oven. That was an excellent way Kerry and I saved me from the panic and probable fire. It's great to have good neighbors, and I bless God for mine!

Chapter 10. Bless and Build Up Your Children

As we discussed in the previous chapter, we need to establish partnership with our children so they can work with us to build up a better future for us and for them. There are certain helpful ways to enable a single mother to establish this partnership with her children. Some points we have mentioned in passing, but I'll go into more detail in this chapter.

Mother, Watch Your Tongue!

As we all know, the tongue is one of the most powerful weapons humans have, especially women. While most abusive men would hit their spouses, the women would lash out with their tongues.

In James 3:1-13, the Bible describes the power of the tongue as '… a fire, a world of iniquity… it defiles the whole body, and sets on fire the course of nature…an unruly evil, full of deadly poison…"!

> ***For in many things we all offend; if any man offend not in word, the same is a perfect man, and able also to bridle the whole body*** *(v2)*
>
> ***Even so the tongue is a little member, and boasts great things; behold how great a matter a little fire kindles!***

> ***And the tongue is a fire, a world of iniquity: so is the tongue among our members, that it defiles the whole body and sets on fire the course of nature; and it is set on fire by hell.*** *(vv. 5-6)*
>
> ***But the tongue can no man tame; it is an unruly evil, full of deadly poison. With it we bless God, even the Father, and with it we curse men who are made in the similitude of God. Out of the same mouth proceeds blessing and cursing. My brethren, these things ought not so to be.*** *(vv. 8-10)*

We're back to the word 'offend' in James 3:2. One of the worst ways in which we offend people, especially those closest to us, our own children, is by our tongues!

I am personally guilty of having used my tongue as a deadly weapon against my kids. But I thank God for rebuking me and fixing my relationship with them. In the heat of anger I used to call them all kinds of nasty names like 'stupid', 'idiot', 'brainless', 'lazy', name it! It's actually very ironic because when my ex called me names, I hated it. To turn around and use the same offense on my children made me a complete contradiction to the things I preached against!

Rather than use angry or hateful words especially when we are angry, the Lord wants us to use words of grace on our children.

> ***There is that speaks like the piercings of a sword; but the tongue of the wise is health*** *(Proverbs 12:18)*
>
> ***Every wise woman builds her house, but the foolish plucks it down with her hands*** *(Proverbs 14:1)*
>
> ***Be ye angry, and sin not; let not the sun go down on your anger... Let no corrupt communication proceed***

> ***out of your mouth, but that which is good for edification, that it may minister grace to the hearers*** *(Ephesians 4:26-29)*

If you begin to speak words of grace to your children instead of hateful words, they'll notice; and as soon as they see that it's a new you, they'll relax, feel safer, and begin to work with you rather than against you. It's only by the power of God, but it is possible.

Adopt a New Strategy: When You're Angry, Bless!

At the recent Encounter program I attended at my church, All Nations, I learnt that children internalize hurts and pains from birth until about 10, when they begin to lash out and rebel against their parents. So by the time your kid begins to lash back at you, it's almost too late, but God can come to the rescue if you work with Him.

Rather than call my children names when they upset me, I've learnt to bless them. I would call the child, lay both hands on his or her head and pray something like,

> ***"Lord, I pray for (child's name); Bless (him); I'm really angry with (him) right now, but bless (him) and give (him) the heart of wisdom to do what is right. I bind the spirit of rebellion and disobedience; I command the spirit of good behavior in this child, in Jesus' Name! Amen!"***

The first time I did this to Emmanuel, my second son, he stepped back and looked at me as if he thought I had gone bananas. He gave me a questioning peek that said, "Mum, are you alright?" He was used to hearing me yell, scream and call him names, and then all of a sudden I'm laying hands on him for not carrying out my specific instructions! That made an impact on him. Did he disobey again? Of course he has many times! Don't we all? But now my kids are more careful to work with me. They know that disobedience won't get under my skin anymore. They know that I would rather lay hands on them and ask God to deal with them, thus handing them over to a superior power: God Himself!

This is not to say that you should ignore your job as disciplinarian. Of course you must discipline your children, but refrain from speaking words that will hurt their spirits.

> ***Death and life are in the power of the tongue, and they that love it shall eat the fruit thereof (Proverbs 18:21)***

When you yell and scream at your children, or call them names, their spirits get angrier and more rebellious, and you achieve nothing. I take that back – you do achieve something: the opposite of what you really want. It's like hitting your head on a brick wall. Moreover, because yelling and name-calling does not ask for divine help, but rather hurts or kills your children's spirits, God cannot help you at that moment; you're entirely on your own. You really don't want to be in that situation with respect to raising children or anything for that matter.

On the other hand, when you combine discipline with laying your hands on them and praying for them, what you're doing is actually asking God to intervene in their lives and in their hearts, to forgive them, and to give them wisdom to behave better. You speak words of grace into their spirits at the time of their offense and the Lord will deal with that spirit of rebellion right away. They actually feel sorrier this way than by yelling and screaming. I definitely prefer this approach.

Get Them Some Father Figures

Let's face facts: there are some things that a woman cannot really do in the life of a child. Personally, I realize that no matter what I do, my children still need their father in their lives. When a child has interaction from both parents, albeit in different settings, the child tends to have more psychological balance than otherwise.

Unfortunately, some people find themselves in a 'dead-beat Dad' situation where the father disappears for reasons best known to him. What should a single mother do in such a case? Give up on your child's father-bonding part? No way!

In Chapter 3 we discussed the need to build a strong community to relate with, not just for you, but also for the children. From this community, it's important to create some father figures for the children. Some people think this is most important for boys, but I find that my girls do really need a father figure too.

At All Nations, I have personally picked out a few men I can trust with my children, who act as Big Brothers or Acting Dad so to say, and their interactions with my children over the past few years have had great positive impact on the children! There are some things those kids discuss with their Big Brothers that I only hear second hand. For example, Uncle Isaac and Uncle Nathaniel have surprised with me with some questions my kids ask them, which they never ask me. Sometimes that makes me jealous, but it only drives home the fact that as my children get older, there are some questions in their minds that they will not ask me, but would rather ask their father or another man.

We cannot overemphasize the children's need for male role models and Big Brothers; men they can look up to and confide in. As your boys grow up, they need men to ask certain biological questions that they would be most highly embarrassed to ask Mum! I have discussed puberty and some sex-related topics with Jerry and Emmanuel, but I know they would feel much more comfortable to discuss these questions with their Big Brothers.

I encourage you to find male role models for your children; this would go a long way to ensuring that they have a more balanced emotional and psychological future ahead of them.

Teach Them The Ways of God

Referring to Chapter 9, our meanings #1 and #4 of the word 'offend' refer to a single mother's responsibility to ***not*** offend her children by transgressing God's law, thereby causing her children to sin.

You have the spiritual responsibility to ***"train up [your] child in the way he should go: and when he is old he will not depart from it"*** (Proverbs 22:6). You cannot afford to leave the training of your child to schools or teachers. An old adage says, 'charity begins at home'. You are your child's foremost teacher. What does a school teacher know of your beliefs for instance? Don't you realize that even the school system has systematized prayer out of schools? What do schools have to offer your child in terms of moral upbringing? These days, it is sufficient to let schools handle the teaching of general and scientific knowledge, but moral upbringing is your responsibility as a parent. If you fail in this responsibility, you transgress divine law, and you would be leading your child into sin and transgression.

Don't leave your children to the madness on television either. Did you know that excessive time spent on television will interfere with their intelligence and performance in school? What kinds of programs do you allow your children to watch on television? Do you realize that those TV programs all have influence on your child's behavior, positively or negatively?

Rather, it's important for your children's future, to expose them rather to the word of God. When they have the solid foundation of the word of God and build up on it, you assure yourself of a sound future generation. Think about your family tree with you as the root and think about the foundation you are laying at that root. If you lay in your children a solid spiritual foundation, they'll pass that on to their children, their children's children, and you'll go down in God's genealogy as a fantastic parent, worthy of emulation. That's what I want for the name 'Rose Joshua' in a genealogical listing!

Bible-Reading Challenge

One way I have been working on my kids is to get them to spend time studying the word of God. During one of our family meetings, we worked out a strategy that has worked quite well for us. I encourage you to try it, and I'm sure your kids will get a good kick out of the exercise.

First, I bought everyone his or her own Bible. This is actually not a big deal because every child should have his or her own Bible anyway, for personal study.

Then we divided the 1189 chapters in the Bible into 52 weeks, which came to about 23 chapters per week.

Then we mapped out a plan whereby they will read through the entire Bible at least once a year, by reading at least 23 chapters a week! It comes to less than 4 chapters a day, which is not a big challenge for a child, not even for my Gabby, who is six years old.

At the end of each week I get them to recount to me what they read (for accountability of course!) and then I pay them their Bible-reading allowance.

Very simple plan and the kids love the reward part at the end of each week. Happily, it actually works much better than I had it planned originally. I found that my children actually want to read much more each week. I find that Jerry and Peace, for instance, compete aggressively with each other, and in the end, they can each read through the entire Bible at least twice a year! Kids love to read! Take advantage of that and give them a Bible-reading challenge. While they are at it, they sow the word of God solidly in their hearts. With a foundation like that, you can never go wrong, because you know that when they grow up, they'll never depart from the teachings of the word of God.

Try it for yourself. What do you spend your own time reading as a grown woman? For me, I let go of some of my favorite soap operas, and I settle down to the word of God instead. I suggest you map out a couple of hours everyday and spend the time chewing on the Bible, so to say. Do you realize you can establish a solid spiritual foundation for yourself and lay a great example for the children in the process? I find that if I read 7 chapters of the Bible everyday, I go through the entire Bible twice in only 340 days. It doesn't even take the whole year! It's quite amazing, but it's an exercise that has worked for me and I'm sure it will work for you.

Having said this, you need to go at your own pace, even if it's a chapter a day. The important point here is to encourage your children to plant the word of God in their hearts. When your children have the word of God in their hearts, you guarantee that they will not be candidates for drugs or crime in the future. There's no better way than that.

Maintain Your Spiritual Hedge By Constant Walk With God

A few years ago, I had a dream in which the kids and I woke up in the middle of the night to the howling of foxes, about a dozen of them! I looked out the window and indeed there was no window at all. It appeared as if the house was completely broken down and we were sleeping directly outside, under the elements. The broken-down walls of our house were all around us! And in that dream there were the foxes heading straight at us for dinner! I quickly gathered the children and I heard a voice that instructed me to run to a friend's home (I do not remember which friend it was in the dream). We ran to that friend's home, and were safe. I woke up with a whisper in my spirit, "Your hedge is broken; your hedge is broken..."

I knew right away what to do. About that time, I had been too busy with work and stress, I had not given myself time to pray. Remember that we need to keep clean and allow the Holy Spirit to continuously maintain a strong defense in us.

Pray with your children daily and teach them to maintain a pattern of constant holy walk with God. In doing this you will be laying a spiritual foundation that no one can take away from them.

Don't leave out discipline!

Does the foregoing exclude discipline? Not at all! Discipline must be part of a child's life or else he would go completely out of control and jail-bound! The word of

God abounds with many direct instructions to discipline your child. Some of them are as follows:

> ***Foolishness is bound in the heart of a child, but the rod of correction shall drive it far from him (Proverbs 22:15)***
>
> ***Chasten your son while there is hope, and let not your soul spare for his crying (Proverbs 19:18)***
>
> ***Correct your son, and he shall give you rest; yes, he shall give delight to your soul (Proverbs 29:17)***
>
> ***As many as I love, I rebuke and chasten… (Revelation 3:19)***

Discipline is therefore good and necessary. In fact, if you don't discipline your children, you offend them as well, because correcting a child is commanded by God Himself!

When you discipline or correct your children, it's because you love them, even as God loves us and disciplines us many times. However, discipline must be implemented in line with God's word. It must not be in such a way as to offend the children as we've discussed previously. We must not crush their spirits or cause them to hate their lives.

No one likes discipline, least of all children, but my approach is to explain to them the good it will do them if I take away privileges here and there, in order to drive home my point, or to remind them to be of good behavior.

You don't do yourself or your children a favor if you refrain from disciplining them. Rather, as the scriptures explain above, if you discipline your child, he would give you rest and bring joy and pride. This therefore implies that if you don't discipline your child, he would bring you shame and dishonor.

> ***The rod and reproof give wisdom: but a child left to himself brings his mother to shame (Proverbs 29:15)***

Who wants to be the mother of a murderer or rapist, for example? No one! Now is the time to lay the foundation in your child's life, by consistent discipline with the love of God.

Keep Them Really Busy In Church, Sports, and Community

What's one of the biggest reasons children get into trouble? Boredom!

Do you realize that your children have lots of talent that could die untapped if you don't dig them out? Unfortunately, rather than channel them towards discovering and developing their talents, we leave them alone to watch television and play all day, everyday! As single mothers, we need to push our children out of the status quo or the mediocre, into a world of excellence and victorious achievements.

Children have lots of stored energy that needs to be burned up. They also have a lot of brain activity that must be employed to use their natural talents effectively. If they don't have the ***right*** things to keep them busy, guess what? Remember that 'foolishness is bound up in the heart of a child' (Proverbs 22:15), and 'a child left to himself will eventually become a shame to his mother' (Proverbs 29:15). If children are left alone and undirected, they would only come up with the wrong, mischievous ideas!

I have five children, whom I call "The Happy Gang". One of the reasons I call them "The Happy Gang" is because by the grace of God, they are mostly happy, but 'gang' because they have so much energy, almost inexhaustible, that if they gang up against you, you simply can't beat them. Most of the ideas in my *Happy Gang Series* are actually from my kids themselves!

My strategy was to come up with activities for my practically indefatigable children, lots of activities! Not so much as to distract their school work, but enough to tire them out and keep them out of trouble each day. That was a challenge, and an expensive venture, but I determined that it was better to pay for sports for example, than to keep them at video games or the television most of the time.

First, I got them involved in church activities; as much as we can, apart from Sunday worship, we attend some weekday activities as well. The boys are learning to drum for the children's church while the girls are in the children's choir and are learning to play the piano. These things keep them focused on the things of God and keep their minds positively busy as well.

On sporting side, Jerry and Emmanuel play indoor soccer or basketball from September through March (the long season) and baseball or soccer from April to June (short season). Peace plays basketball in the long season, and outdoor soccer in the short season, while Faith and Gabby play basketball or indoor soccer in the long season and outdoor soccer in the short season. Throughout the year, they all swim as well! So each child is involved in at least two sporting activities all the time.

It's a lot of driving around and expenses for me, but I thank God for the great neighbors and coaches I have, who readily volunteer to pick up and drop off kids for me when schedules conflict. For example, Kerry and Dave's son, Mitchell, has been in the same baseball team with Jerry the past two years. Kerry volunteered to take Jerry to ***all*** his baseball games, whether I can make it or not! Without neighbors and coaches like that, I couldn't possibly make it to all the children's activities.

The bottom-line is to keep your children really busy. For example, if your child comes home from school at 3:45pm, and has ballet or soccer at 6:00pm, that leaves only enough time to do her homework, play for about half an hour, eat a quick snack, shower and get ready for the activity, go for her activity from 6-8pm, come home, and get ready for bed! In that time, where will the child have the time to get into trouble? Of course there's time to play because their activities are not everyday, but your child will generally be busy enough to stay out of trouble. That's my strategy, and so far, I've found it very effective.

Furthermore, involvement in church and sports is great for the kids because they get many benefits from them. They learn great skills including:

sportsmanship,

teamwork,

social relationships,

communication skills,

planning skills

plus they get lots and lots of fun and exercise!

It's a lot of reward for the money you pay for their sporting activities. As for the cost, I know that communities do have subsidies for families who have low income, so if cost is a problem, enquire and you may be happily surprised. For example, our swimming center has 'single-parent family' rates, which cuts my membership cost there by about 20%. It's good to take advantage of these community provisions.

There are several talents that your children may have which are left undeveloped. Many of them love music; take them to piano or guitar classes. Let them compose songs and record them into their own cassettes. Who knows, you may have budding musicians right under your nose! So find out what your children's talents are, take them to where they can develop those talents and keep them as busy and away from trouble as possible.

Chores: Don't Kill Yourself!

How about chores? Do you find that you're working so hard everyday and the place is a mess right after you clean up, and you are in a cycle of 'clean-up' all the time while the kids are in the opposite mess-up cycle?

I used to overwork myself with house chores until my Mum told me I was slowly committing suicide! So I got the kids involved. Rather than restrict their chores only to cleaning their rooms, I expanded chores to include the whole house, plus dishes, and laundry, everything. Also, rather than have a cleaning lady over once a month, I decided to get everyone to clean their assigned space at least twice a week. And it works! These days, when I come into the house and it's like a tornado hit it, I know that it will be all tidy again when we do our one-hour cleanup.

The results for me have been that the kids are involved in the housework and I am not as fatigued as I used to be. They take pride in their work; they police it themselves, and they know that if they mess it up, ***they*** clean it up.

The other thing I have done is to establish a dish-cleaning routine, which we've been doing for about two years now. Every kid has his/her day to do the dishes. I have a dishwasher that I don't use frequently, because I want my children to learn to do the dishes. It's more talking and reminding work for me, but in the end they are learning to be more responsible around the house.

Also, I teach each child to cook. Jerry and Emmanuel have days when it's "boys' turn" to cook and they come up with really interesting meals sometimes! The girls have their own turns as well. At ages 11 and under, my kids can cook practically every meal they eat in the house, from rice and pasta to deserts! They have difficulty with some of my local dishes, but they can cook sauces from scratch, bake from scratch, and if you give them an uncomplicated recipe, they can follow it. They can cook and bake unassisted, but I watch for any potential fire hazards around the oven (you never know with kids). The good thing about teaching them to cook is that some days when I'm really exhausted, I ask them to come up with something for dinner, and they do a great job! They take pride in their cooking, and feel really good about themselves. It's quite rewarding.

My idea for getting the kids heavily involved in house chores is to not fatigue myself out everyday. With a daytime/full-time paid job and my evening/full-time unpaid "Mum the Driver" job, I need all the help I can around the house. I encourage you to do the same with your children. They'll grow up being more responsible, better future husbands and wives, and you'll be more rested on a regular basis.

Teach Them To Save

Have you ever been out shopping with the kids and they want this, and they want that, and that, and … they want practically the whole store? I have. I think this identifies with most kids. They want every toy, every candy, every pop; it's quite interesting. Sometimes, if they don't get their way, they even throw a tantrum in the store!

It's important to teach your children about focusing on what they ***need***, not what they ***want***. If we all bought what we *wanted*, we would all end up living on "#1 Poverty Avenue". For me, it was a difficult and still ongoing process, but I think my children understand that Mum's income is not unlimited, that we have to focus first on tithes, food, mortgage and bills, and other things can be purchased on a *need* basis. If it's not *necessary*, I won't buy it. Sometimes they hate that, but it's a good lesson for them to learn, and they'll be grateful for this when they grow up.

Get your children involved in your investment and College Fund savings program. When they see the money grow, they get more into saving. Every month when my kids see their RESP statements, they get so excited, and they want to give me their savings to add to it. Sometimes I hear them telling their friends how much money they have in their College funds!

Get Them To Think About The Future

You notice that my Personal Progress / Pickup Challenge is based on the things you wanted when you were a child.

Children have very imaginative minds, which should be channeled to help them form plans for their futures. If you get children to start thinking about what they want to be when they grow up, it would help you to channel them more effectively. If they come up with ideas that you think may not be of benefit to them, you can slowly assist their thinking to more beneficial directions. Don't shut them up or tell them what to do, but discuss with them and guide them into helpful thought patterns.

One thing that helps my children to plan for the future is their RESP or College Fund. They know that Mum is saving up for their College education, and so they're thinking of what they would like to study in College, although they're all still in elementary school. For example, since Jerry got his prescription glasses two years ago, he's been saying he wants to be an Ophthalmologist! What I've done then is to get him library books on the subject of eyes and their internal structure, and other medical books that will help him research Ophthalmology. It's still a long way, and maybe he'll be an Ophthalmologist, maybe not. My part is to encourage him to think about the future.

Sometimes I get my children to draw me a picture of how their house will be when they grow up. They come up with beautiful sketches, with pools and backyard tennis courts and fancy stuff. Then we take the pictures and discuss mortgages and what it means to invest in a house, monthly payments, home expenses and so on. Eventually we always get around to education because to make the money for mortgage, they must have good education and good jobs. So their minds are thinking about these things, and thinking about positive ways to achieve their dreams as they grow up. I believe that's quite positive for them, and will help channel their minds towards using their time and talents more productively than otherwise.

Each child has a bright future ahead of him or her. Our job as mothers is to steer them into that bright future with the help of all the tools around us. May God help us to succeed.

Chapter 11. Forgive – For Your Own Sake

In this chapter, let us discuss a very important aspect of our personal welfare that has very high impact on the physical, spiritual and psychological welfare of ourselves and our children – forgiveness. The target here is the person who has wronged you – your ex, or your children's father. We will discuss forgiveness from a benefits perspective, your benefit that is.

What is Forgiveness?

I've paraphrased the Merriam-Webster' Dictionary meaning of the word *forgiveness* as follows:

to stop feeling anger, annoyance, resentment, or bitterness, against someone who has wronged you;

to give up your claim for requital for an offense against you

the word *requital* used in meaning #2 means "something given or demanded in return, a compensation, retaliation, or vengeance", which implies that *forgiveness* involves giving up on a desire for retaliation or vengeance

Forgiveness is the putting away of anger, bitterness and resentment against my ex-husband. This means that when someone mentions his name, or when I see him or hear his voice, the proof that I have forgiven him is that my stomach does not knot up in an angry twist! It is difficult to forgive but it's possible with the strength of God. Now that I have forgiven my ex, I see him as one who desperately needs help and no longer as the one who upset or abused me. He is the one I need to feel sorry for because I've handed him over to my Father God to deal with.

The Lord demonstrates His love to us when He forgives and deliberately refuses to remember our iniquities. The Lord says of His children:

> ***For I will be merciful to their unrighteousness, and their sins and their iniquities will I remember no more (Hebrews 8:12)***

Unforgiveness is a spirit that fights and yells into our hearts, "There's no way you can ever forgive that jerk! Think about all the things he did to you!" You need to get that spirit cast away from you forever, because in forgiving us our sins, God Himself leaves us an example to do the same.

Why Do We Need To Forgive?

Essentially, for our own sakes. As a single mother left all alone to cater for my five children physically, emotionally and financially, I need to forgive their father, for ***my own sake***, not his! There are several reasons we need to forgive and forget.

First, the Lord commands it. In the gospels, you find that if you do not forgive someone who has offended you, you deceive yourself when you go to the heavenly Father in prayer.

> ***"For if you forgive men their trespasses, your heavenly Father will also forgive you. But if you do not forgive men their trespasses, neither will your Father forgive your trespasses." (Matthew 6:14, 15)***

> ***"And whenever you stand praying, if you have anything against anyone, forgive him, that your Father in heaven may also forgive you your trespasses. But if you do not forgive, neither will your Father in heaven forgive your trespasses." Mark 11:25, 26.***

As a matter of fact, victory in prayer starts with your forgiving your offenders. Mark 11:25-26 is preceded by Mark 11:23-24, which declares God's readiness to move your mountains, and to do anything you ask in prayer, but you must forgive first:

> ***For verily I say to you, that whosoever shall say to this mountain, be removed and be cast into the sea, and shall not doubt in his heart, but shall believe that those things he says shall come to pass, he shall have whatsoever he says. Therefore I say to you, what things soever you desire, when you pray, believe that you receive them, and you shall have them. And whenever you pray, forgive, if you have anything against anyone...*** *(Mark 11: 23-26)*

So you see that your victory in life is tied to your forgiving anyone who has wronged you, especially your ex.

Secondly, vengeance belongs to God. For some reason, Jesus directs us to ***'love our enemies, and pray for those who despitefully use us'*** *(Matthew 5:44)*. I used to wonder about that scripture, until I saw Paul's explanation in Romans 12:

> ***Dearly beloved, avenge not yourselves, but rather give place to wrath, for it is written, "Vengeance is mine", says the Lord. Therefore if your enemy is hungry, feed him; if he is thirsty, give him drink, for in so doing, you shall heap coals of fire on his head. Do not be overcome by evil, but overcome evil with good*** *(Romans 12:19-21)*

These days, I find that when I pray for my ex, that it may be well with him for the children's sakes, I feel much better within myself, knowing that I have released him to God.

You see, when you take vengeance and anger upon yourself, you declare to God that you want to fight this battle on your own. But when you forgive and let go, you put God on your side and He fights for you against your enemies.

Before I learnt this secret, I hated my ex so much, I wished he would drop dead, literally! But now, knowing that the Lord will set a table before me in the presence of my enemies, I am praying that God will let him live long so he can see the goodness of God upon my life! Now I use my spiritual energy differently!

Medical Reasons To Forgive!

Moreover, medical scientists have proven that anger, bitterness and unforgiveness are connected to potentially terminal illnesses like cancer, hypertension, arteriosclerosis, and ulcers.

For example, medical studies by Goldfarb (1989), Lafond (1988), and Oppenheimer (1987, 1991) describe the science of the cause of cancer:

> ***"... scientists believe that genetic changes, whether inherited or acquired, are the basic cause of cancer. Some scientific theories do suggest that cancer may be a hereditary disease because each individual's make-up may make them more susceptible to certain cancers. About 50 of the more than 120 different types of cancer occasionally run in families.***
>
> ***(However,) most of the current scientific evidence indicates that a normal cell can become transformed into a cancer cell when certain genes become activated. Recent work in cancer biology concerns the study of oncogenes, a specific gene that participates in changing a normal cell into a cancer cell. It is thought that an oncogene might be present in an inactive form in normal cells and is some way activated to create cancer cells."***

My understanding from the above is that even if one is naturally not susceptible genetically to cancer, that person could *acquire* susceptibility by allowing events that transform and activate normal body cells into cancer cells.

Furthermore, Ernest H. Johnson, an Associate Professor of Psychology at the University of Miami and the Behavioral Medicine Research Program, wrote a book titled ***"The Deadly Emotions: The Role of Anger,***

Hostility, and Aggression in Health and Emotional Well-Being" (1990), reviewed as follows:

> ***" ... establishes a link between emotions and health. In this book, Professor Johnson suggests a potentially deadly role for anger, hostility, and aggression (AHA syndrome) in several health problems including heart disease, cancer, ulcers, and hypertension. He also explores the relationship between AHA syndrome and psychological problems such as depression, chronic stress, smoking, drinking, and child/spouse abuse."***

Grunbaum et al. (1997) establish a clear association between anger and hostility and the risk of coronary heart disease, and Matthews et al. (1998, 1999) have established that "suppressed anger increases the risk of heart disease by as much as 75%"!!!

Probably one of the most vivid descriptions I have read on this subject was done by Dr. Redford Williams, a medical Professor at Duke University. In his book ***"Anger kills",*** Dr. Williams warns that ***people who maintain high anger levels are seven times more likely to be dead of heart disease by age 50!*** A review of his book states:

> ***"... those with hostile personalities are stressing their bodies out by calling on them over and over again to go into "fight or flight" mode -- in essence putting the body on alert to handle external attacks ... the chronic use of this response over time may cause degradation of the whole body: cardiovascular, immune system, stomach, you name it.."***

Dr. Williams further explains that

> ***"...the body prepares itself to handle a perceived threat, such as a job conflict or traffic stress, in the same way it prepares for an actual physical attack. The brain***

> ***releases the hormone** noradrenalin **directly into the heart, causing it to work up to five times harder than normal. Meanwhile, the diameter of blood vessels throughout the body decreases, forcing blood into muscles and raising blood pressure dramatically… all of these changes help your body function at optimum capacity in an actual life-threatening situation. On the other hand, if you're merely sitting in traffic or waiting in a supermarket line, all these changes still take place, but serve no useful function."***

Williams' research also showed that

> ***"... when a person gets angry, fat is released into his bloodstream. If it isn't burned off through exercise, the fat will simply turn into cholesterol..."***

In a layman's language, a state of anger causes the body to secrete bile-like toxins into the blood stream, toxins which work against blood flow, hemoglobin formation, and a consequential weakening of the body's defense / immune system. And this leads to deadly diseases like depression, high blood pressure, even cancer! When I read these things, I doubled up my efforts to forgive my ex and to stop bitterness against him as soon as possible!

Also, after reading the medical analysis of anger and hostility, I realized that when the Bible says I should forgive, it is more for my own sake, than for the sake of those who have offended me.

Think about this: sometimes people actually forget that they even said anything nasty to you! They go about their business as if nothing happened (as a matter of fact, to them, nothing happened)! And there you are, fuming and pining away, just because you can't forgive them!

What an irony: that sometimes, the person who ends up suffering the most is the innocent victim, simply because she won't forgive!

Get Rid of Bitterness – Quick!

As we see from medical research above, anger and bitterness are evil cankerworms that eat into our physical and spiritual defense systems, and rob us of our salvation, our health, and our eternal rewards.

I thank God for my Senior Pastor, Dr. Donkor, who helped me deal with the spirit of bitterness, unforgiveness and resulting depression!

When I first got to All Nations, I kept away from the Pastor and many of the men generally. In my cultural language, we have an adage that says, "A person who has been bitten by a rabid dog, runs from even a one-day-old puppy". It's our way of saying, "once bitten, twice shy", but our adages are somewhat more graphical than English proverbs. Anyway, I did keep away from Dr. Donkor. Of course, I ran into him many times, and chatted, but I was mentally aloof. However, one day, after discussing with Mama Rose, she encouraged me to go and talk to the Senior Pastor. So I went.

Pastor Donkor recognized right away that I was wrestling with the spirit of depression. He also saw that I had a lot of bitterness and unforgiveness in my heart. He opened the scriptures to me, and explained my need to forgive my ex. He prayed with me, and along with Prayer

Pastor Sammy Akoi and the then Regional Touch Pastor Joe Armson, cast out the demons of depression and bitterness, and I was set free!

In Hebrews 12:14-15, we are told to:

> ***Follow peace with all men, and holiness without which no man shall see the Lord: looking diligently lest any man fail of the grace of God; lest any root of bitterness springing up troubles you, and thereby many be defiled.***

When you allow bitterness to dwell in your spirit against your ex or anyone, ***you*** are the one who will get sick and depressed, ***you*** are the one who will go to hell!

My people have an adage that says:

> ***'A wrestler holding his opponent down on the ground is also holding himself down'***

True. Do you know that it takes energy to stay angry, and that is negative energy that destroys your spirit and body? As long as you don't forgive and forget and you remain angry, you spend your precious emotional and mental energy planning how to get back at him, somebody who doesn't even care or remember that he hurt you! If you release that anger and forgive, you release yourself to begin to spend your emotional and mental energy on improving yourself and moving forward, as we have discussed in this book.

You have lots of mental capacity. You've got to choose to use it wisely and positively by forgiving. As the wrestler holding his opponent on the ground, you're declared the true winner when you release him, and stand up in victory! That victory is achieved by forgiveness.

Forgiveness and Future Dating Relationships

Note also that the victory of forgiveness will enable you to put the past behind you and to work on future relationships.

For example, if you are considering remarrying, you will need to forgive your ex so you won't transfer your anger to your new husband. If you carry the baggage of unforgiveness into a new marriage and your new husband does something similar to your ex, you might find yourself flaring up out of proportion. It's important to clean up the past and look to the future objectively.

I spoke to my Pastors about the issue of divorced Christians remarrying. They confirm the Bible's position that God's ideal is that divorces not take place. However, if you're divorced, it's better to remarry than to live in fornication or adultery or to fool around from man to man like a harlot. As the word of God says in I Corinthians 7:8-9,

> ***I say therefore to the unmarried and widows, it is good for them if they abide even as I. But if they cannot contain, let them marry: for it is better to marry than to burn.***

It's better to marry than to burn. So it may be a good idea to remarry if you find that you're excessively lonely. However, it's very important that you take time to study your new husband and deal with him as a *separate* individual than your ex. Avoid punishing your new husband for the sins of your ex. Truly forgive your ex, so you can move on with your new life and enjoy it!

Chapter 12. Finally, Be a Woman On a Mission!

Proverbs 31: 10-31:

> ***Who can find a virtuous woman? For her price is far above rubies. The heart of her husband doth safely trust in her, so that he shall have no need of spoil. She will do him good and not evil all the days of her life. She seeks wool, and flax, and works willingly with her hands. She is like the merchants' ships; she brings her food from afar. She rises also while it is yet night, and gives food her household, and a portion to her maidens. She considers a field and buys it: with the fruit of her hands she plants a vineyard. She girds her loins with strength, and strengthens her arms. She perceives that her merchandise is good: her candle goes not out by night. She lays her hand to the spindle, and her hands hold the distaff. She stretches out her hand to the poor; yes, she reaches forth her hands to the needy. She is not afraid of the snow for her household: for all her household are clothed with scarlet. She makes herself coverings of tapestry; her clothing is silk and purple. Her husband is known in the gates, when he sits among the elders of the land. She makes fine linen, and sells it; and delivers girdles to the merchant. Strength and honor are her clothing; and she shall rejoice in time to come. She opens her mouth with wisdom; and in her tongue is the law of kindness. She looks well to the ways of her household, and eats not the bread of idleness. Her children arise up and call her blessed; her husband also, and he praises her. Many daughters have done virtuously, but you excel them all. Favor is deceitful, and beauty is vain: but a woman that fears the Lord, she shall be praised. Give her of the fruit of her hands; and let her own works praise her in the gates.***

I wrap up this book by challenging every single mother, and in fact, every mother, to strive to be a woman on a mission! Say to yourself: “I am a woman on a mission”.

What is your mission?

> ***I pledge to be the best mother I can be, to raise my children in the best possible manner, to be the best they can be to God and country, so help me God!***

As a single mother, my mission is to protect my children from harm, show them God’s way, pray with them, and teach them to become the role models and leaders of tomorrow.

My mission is to ensure that my children will not be counted in the negative statistics of ‘children from broken homes’. In fact, my mission is to change the world’s view of ‘children from broken homes’ from a negative view to a positive one. I must strive to ensure that although my children are from a so-called broken home, they are not broken in themselves! My mission is to build in each of them a solid foundation, a solid and balanced personality, love for themselves, the fear of God, respect of others, and a mission in their own hearts to be good and top examples that must be emulated!

This is my mission! This is my declaration to them as a mother. And this is my challenge to every single mother in the world!

The Mission of a Virtuous Woman

God would have us turn around the lives of our children from the norm of expected failure, to the victory of successful children brought up by the collaboration of God and the hosts of heaven and a praying mother.

God has given us the roadmap in the life of 'the virtuous woman' as described in Proverbs 31. In this chapter, I'd like to analyze the 'virtuous woman' and relate her to myself, and to my role as mother and future wife if applicable.

v10: Who can find a virtuous woman? For her price is far above rubies.

My mission is that I, as a woman, will be respected and valued in my society. I will not be a bum. I will not place myself in a position where I could become a reproach or an object of ridicule. My price must be far above rubies. I will take my place as a mother in society and as a respectable role model.

vv11-12: The heart of her husband doth safely trust in her, so that he shall have no need of spoil. She will do him good and not evil all the days of her life.

My mission is that if I ever remarry, my husband will count himself very blessed to have me as his wife. I'll do him good and he will rely on me and trust in me because he will recognize that I have the character, skills, and capability to be a dependable woman. My mission is to build in myself that dependable character that can be vouched for anywhere.

vv13-15: She seeks wool, and flax, and works willingly with her hands. She is like the merchants' ships; she brings her food from afar. She rises also while it is yet night, and gives food her household, and a portion to her maidens.

My mission is to not allow myself to be lazy. Knowing that God hates laziness, and "***the hand of the diligent shall bear rule, but the slothful shall be under tribute***" (Proverbs 12:24), I will not be lazy. I will work with my hands willingly. I will plan my affairs ahead of time. I will not be caught sleeping when I should be up and about. I will not allow myself to become a couch potato because that's bad example for my children. My mission is to not allow myself to spend precious time watching excessive television and wasting hours that could otherwise be spent being productive both for myself and for my children.

vv16-19: She considers a field and buys it: with the fruit of her hands she plants a vineyard. She girds her loins with strength, and strengthens her arms. She perceives that her merchandise is good: her candle goes not out by night. She lays her hand to the spindle, and her hands hold the distaff.

My mission is to invest in my future and the futures of my children. I will not allow myself to be unfocused or to lack a plan or vision for my life. I will strengthen myself, and plant and sow into my children's education. I will plant and sow into their morals, and into their success in their generation. I will spare nothing to invest in my children and I will establish in them the seed of success.

v20: She stretches out her hand to the poor; yes, she reaches forth her hands to the needy.

My mission is to place myself in a position where I can give to the poor. This means that I must not be poor myself. This means that I will do everything possible to gain the knowledge, abilities and positions that will give me the opportunities to give. According to the word of God, I will not be a borrower but a lender, according to God's prosperity. My mission is to lay a giving foundation for my children, and to teach them to be the givers of tomorrow. Therefore, as givers, they will not be lazy themselves and will work to lay up so they can give.

vv21-25: She is not afraid of the snow for her household: for all her household are clothed with scarlet. She makes herself coverings of tapestry; her clothing is silk and purple. Her husband is known in the gates, when he sits among the elders of the land. She makes fine linen, and sells it; and delivers girdles to the merchant. Strength and honor are her clothing; and she shall rejoice in time to come.

My mission is to clothe my children in honor. My children will not look haggard. They will not be unkempt. They will be respected by their friends, by their peers, and by everyone who comes across them. This is not to say that I will spend my time and hard-earned money on vogue items. I will rather ensure that they are well clad, feel confident in themselves, without being foolish or extravagant. In so doing I will teach them to be wise in their own spending, and to prioritize between needs and wants.

v26-27: She opens her mouth with wisdom; and in her tongue is the law of kindness. She looks well to the ways of her household, and eats not the bread of idleness.

My mission is to be a woman whom people will seek after for words of wisdom, and for direction. I will speak words of encouragement and peace, with honest criticism where it's called for. I will teach my children to speak with wisdom. My children will comport and conduct themselves like ladies and gentlemen. They will not spend their time unwisely in idleness or things that do not benefit them. They will speak to others with politeness and polishing, and they will pave ways for themselves with their words of wisdom.

vv28-31: Her children arise up and call her blessed; her husband also, and he praises her. Many daughters have done virtuously, but you excel them all. Favor is deceitful, and beauty is vain: but a woman that fears the Lord, she shall be praised. Give her of the fruit of her hands; and let her own works praise her in the gates.

My mission is to ensure that my children are proud to be my children. They will be proud to say, "That's my Mum!" They will be proud to be associated with me. My mission is that if I remarry, my husband will be proud of me, and will *honestly* praise me, not only in my presence but also in my absence! My mission is that people will see in me the beauty of God, and praise God because of what they see Him doing in my life.

In Conclusion...

And so, I am indeed a woman on a mission, and I challenge you to set yourself on a mission as well. Here's a simplified version of my mission statement:

I am a woman on a mission

I refuse to be distracted

I refuse to be intimidated
I refuse to allow myself to be idle
I will establish a plan and a vision

I will roll up my sleeves and work

I will build my house in strength

I will not live in laziness or procrastination

I will clothe my household in honor and dignity

My children will call me blessed

This is not a mission impossible

It is possible with God's help
I will succeed with God's help
And so shall it be, in Jesus' Name;

Amen and Amen!!

You see, you have so much potential in you that if you start digging it out right now, you would be shocked at what you can do! But it's impossible without focus or without a vision of what you want to be tomorrow. You need a mission, a reason and a motivation to keep going. I pray that as you focus on the goodness of God, and walk with Him daily, He will give you the grace and strength to be a woman on a mission.

I challenge you to move on in a 'mission possible'. As a single mother, you have a challenge ahead of you, but it's not an impossible task. It is possible as you put your hands in the Hands of the One who sees tomorrow, who alone can lead you through the wilderness. He has given you the victory already. All you need to do is take that victory and move on with your life, into success!

Remember: ***you can do all things through Christ who will daily give you strength*** (Philippians 4:13). May God bless you and your children, Amen.

References

Merriam Webster (2003). *Online Dictionary.* http://www.m-w.com/, @ July 2003.

Goldfarb, Ronald H. (Ed.) (1989). Cancer Growth and Progression Volume 1 (November 1989): Fundamental Aspects of Cancer. Norwell, MA: Kluwer Academic Publishers. 214pp.

Lafond, Richard (1988). *Cancer: The Outlaw Cell.* Washington, D.C.: American Chemical Society. 289pp.

Oppenheimer, Steven B. (1987). Advances in Cancer Biology, *The American Biology Teacher*, January 1987, pp.11-15.

Oppenheimer, Steven B. (1991). "Tumor Suppressor Genes: A Key to the Cancer Puzzle?" *The American Biology Teacher,* January 1991, pp. 22-24.

Grunbaum, Jo Anne; Vernon, Sally; and Clasen Carla M. (1997). "The association between anger and hostility and risk factors for coronary heart disease in children and adolescents: A review", The University of Texas-Houston Health Science Center. (*Ann. Behav. Med.* 19(2):179-189.

Benschop, Robert J; Geenen, Rinie; Mills, Paul J; Naliboff, Bruce D; Kiecolt-Glaser, Janice K; Herbert, Tracy B; van der Pompe, Gieta; Miller, Gregory E;

Matthews, Karen A; Godaert, Guido L R; Gilmore, Stephanie L; Glaser, Ronald; Heijnen, Cobi J; Dopp, Joel M; Bijlsman, Johannes W J; Solomon, George F; Cacioppo, John T. (1998) : Cardiovascular and Immune Responses to Acute Psychological Stress in Young and Old Women: A Meta-Analysis, *Psychosom. Med.* 60(3): 290-296.

Matthews, Karen A; Gump, Brooks B; Block, Diana R; Allen, Michael T (1997): Does Background Stress Heighten or Dampen Children's Cardiovascular Responses to Acute Stress?, *Psychosom. Med.* 59(5): 488-496.

Matthews, Karen A; Owens, Jane F; Kuller, Lewis H; Sutton-Tyrrell, Kim; Jansen-McWilliams, Linda (1998): Are Hostility and Anxiety Associated With Carotid Atherosclerosis in Healthy Postmenopausal Women?, *Psychosom. Med.* 60(5): 633-638

Williams, Redwood and Williams, Virginia(1998); Anger Kills : Seventeen Strategies for Controlling the Hostility That Can Harm Your Health. HarperCollins Publishers. 368pp.